Under the Same FLAG

A Journey Through the Odds

GG Elizabeth Mata

ISBN 978-1-954345-69-0 (paperback)
ISBN 978-1-954345-70-6 (hardcover)
ISBN 978-1-954345-71-3 (digital)

Copyright © 2021 by GG Elizabeth Mata

All rights reserved. No part of this publication may be reproduced, distributed, or transmitted in any form or by any means, including photocopying, recording, or other electronic or mechanical methods without the prior written permission of the publisher. For permission requests, solicit the publisher via the address below.

Rushmore Press LLC
1 800 460 9188
www.rushmorepress.com

Printed in the United States of America

Prologue

I stepped out of the glass building on Howard Hughes Center holding my suitcase in one hand and my victory in the other. I had just closed my biggest commercial transaction—a victory that did not come easy, a victory that started in a humble foreign country and against all odds. I could only think of two reasons for my success, God and this wonderful country that gave me the opportunity. As I'm standing outside, I look to the sky to thank my God, and there she was, dancing in the sky full of pride and freedom, representing what many only hope to have one day: the magnificent American flag.

1

The American Flag

I pictured the American flag dancing with the wind in all its glory as my mother was telling us that we were moving to the United States; I had just turned seven years old.

I thought of the United States as the ultimate place to live; it had everything we did not have! Disneyland, Theaters, Hollywood—I mean that is where all the cool stuff came from like Mattel toys, Nike sneakers, and nice clothes! And every time my father visited, he would bring us the best clothes, shoes, and toys in the whole block. If your dad was in the United States, you were a cool kid. I only dreamed and hoped to one day live there.

There was a sense of hope, something to look forward to.

Everyone has a story.

I was born in 1982, in Lagos de Moreno, Jalisco, Mexico. It was a very small, quaint town that seemed as if it was frozen in a colonial era. The roads were made out of stone and mud, and the town was adorned with Catholic parish churches—the stamp of an era conquered by the Spanish conquistadores. Romantic small parks that surround the parishes was a sign that religion and family was once very highly valued in this town. The older women still wore dresses past the knees with aprons; and men wore dress shirts, cowboy hats, and boots. It was a very conservative town.

My mother had built and designed our little home, while my father sent her the money to complete it. It was a two-story townhouse with two bedrooms and a loft. She painted our home a bright pink color. She was very proud of this accomplishment.

My mother had three miscarriages before she had me. I was very well expected, prayed for, and wished for when I was born, as the threat of miscarriage still lingered. Everyone says I was their little doll, with huge eyelashes and tons of silky black hair and chubby pink cheeks, weighing in almost twelve pounds.

Being the youngest and also being a rainbow baby, you are treated a bit more spoiled. You are just a little bit more cared for, especially since it took so much effort for my mother to have me. Everyone liked to call me Lupita, and I enjoyed the spotlight by all my aunts and family. I was a born leader and had so much confidence as a toddler and preschooler. My cousins Carlitos and Adrian would come and play, and usually it was me who was calling the shots. They were always at my house playing, and I would often make a deal with them so they can do my shores. I didn't realize that it was called employing someone to do a task; after all, I was just five.

I had two best friends, Karla and Erica. They lived across the street from me, and I would play with them at their house from daylight until the nighttime. Karla was just a few years older than me, and Erica was just around my age. Their house was huge compared to mine and had so many hiding places. They were the youngest of their siblings. We did everything together. Karla, being the oldest, was always teaching us different games we could play. Funny how, with virtually no toys, we had so much fun, allowing our imagination to take the lead.

I had a very normal happy childhood my first years of life. I enjoyed and rejoiced in my happy memories when we camped with *abuela* and had flower offerings to the Virgin Mary. We had so many field trips with my mother's family. Má Angelita (abuela) was very much a strict Catholic and would take us to church and all the above ceremonies every single legitimate Catholic would do. I admired her so much for how strong she was and how good she was at keeping all of the family together and creating such great memories.

But Má Pabla was my backbone. She had eight daughters and two sons. My father was her rock, being the oldest of the males. They all viewed my father as the glue of the family, and in Hispanic traditions, the oldest male of the family is seen as the father figure, if the father is absent or has passed away. Therefore, since my father passed away when I was only five years old, he is respected and viewed as the father figure. Today, he is still very much respected. When I was born, I had my father's curls; and my grandmother, being right next door to my house, was always caring for me and showing me off all over town.

Má Pabla was a very strong woman with a very strong character but was more easygoing. She didn't take crap from anyone, had no hairs in her tongue, a dirty mouth, and a very good sense of humor. She was a great cook and could really throw some great parties. I could smell Má Pabla making fresh tortillas on the open fire on the griddle from my house and would often sneak out to her house to eat and play. Most houses in my town had an interior patio; and the bedrooms, kitchen, and living rooms often had the entrance door on the interior corridor patio. So every time grandmother cooked, we could smell her food from my house.

I remember my last birthday prior to leaving my hometown. By now, I had become a very different child than that confident, mischievous five-year-old child I used to be. I was turning seven years old at that time. My mother was doing a birthday party for me, and I was more excited about my gifts: a pair of underwear, ruffled socks, and undershirts. I was grateful.

Times were hard, but I didn't understand what being poor meant because my mother always managed to bring happiness in our childhood. She had fair skin with freckles and gorgeous brown, wavy hair from my grandfather's Spanish background. She was a rebel and a fighter. I always viewed my mother as the most beautiful mom in the world. She ran every morning to maintain her shape. She liked to smoke and wear tighter-than-needed clothes.

I would always hear complaints about my mom dressing a lot less modest than a married woman should, but she was young and very good looking, and frankly, she never cared what others think. My mother, like my father, was the glue of her family and everyone always respected her in her family. She was known to be tough, determined, and a problem solver. My mother had been taking care of us for a while with the little she had as my father had left to United States in hopes for a better future, but my mother started struggling and seemed to be always on the edge. She grew up without a father.

Grandpa was a ladies' man and left my grandmother with ten children. My mother had a really tough childhood. She started working at a very young age and would tell me stories on how she never owned a doll made out of plastic. They were too poor, so instead her dolls were made out of straw. She did what she could to give us a better childhood, even giving up her dream of becoming a nurse. I could understand why she was determined to have us grow up with a father, no matter what. The memories of her childhood were all too hapless.

She was pulling it all together, but lately, for the most part, we barely had enough to eat. A roll of bread with eggs for lunch and beans with tortillas for dinner was usual and normal. How nice it was to have sandwiches as it was rare and costly; it was a special day when we made a trip to the deli to buy fresh ham and cheese.

My father would visit us once a year. I could hardly remember him every time he came. On one of his visits, I told my father, "Daddy, while you were gone, there was a man with a beard that visited mommy." And my father just laughed.

My father had let his beard grow the last time he visited, they later explained. When I looked at my father, I felt safe and I felt protected. I loved him. He would often bring me toys. Those were the happiest times of the year. We would go on trips to the mountains and have a lot of get-togethers when he visited as he was the novelty in the small town.

They were also the darkest times as he would hurt my mother. I would hide behind the couch whenever they started fighting, terrified and hurt from his rage and physical abuse. My mother had bought me a kid-sized bench. It was only a few days when she bought it for me when my father picked it up and threw it against my mother until it was broken. At that moment, I never looked at my father the same way again. My mother would then take it out on us after he left. I would often run to Má Pabla's house to hide.

One day, Má Pabla had let me and my cousins make a quick trip to the market across the highway. It was normal for small children to cross the highway to the store because often children are expected to help in the household by either cleaning or doing errands at a very early age. We all held hands on our way back, running across. We didn't catch a light blue Ford truck heading straight at me. In an attempt to save my life, the truck swerved to the right, missing half my body and scrapping my left shoulder.

The impact tossed me and took my skin with it. The truck ended up slamming into a tree, and the poor man seemed to be okay. But I could see that he was terrified that he might have killed me if he didn't turn. The pain was horrible; it felt like I had just burned my shoulder. As soon as my grandma saw me, she sat me on her kitchen table and began rinsing my arm with a small bucket and then put ointment on my arm and wrapped it.

We heard the yelling as someone had run to tell mother that I had been run over. My Má Pabla and I interlocked eyes as if we both knew both of us were in trouble, and then Má Pabla quickly hid me in a closet. I heard them arguing back and forth. Mother opened the closet. I could see how furious she was as she took a tight grip of the sandal and began hitting me as hard as she could. Good news is, my left shoulder didn't hurt as much as her beating; bad news is, I was sore for days.

Her beatings were usually like this. Her way to discipline was calamitous. But we all loved our mother very much. She was, is, and will always be my everything.

It seemed that was her only way to discipline. As a matter a fact, it seemed that was the norm everywhere, including school. I often would receive beatings at school with a ruler from my teachers. Discipline seemed to be the priority. Everyone knew that once the teachers asked you to pull out your hands, you were getting hit with the ruler.

Since the day I got ran over and my mother beat me, I refrained from telling my mother anything at all. I was more scared of my mother than anything that could happen to me outside my house. I was extremely quiet as a child and tremulous. I often sat at school during recess to avoid talking or interacting with anyone. I was an introvert. I built walls around me so that nobody could get in and hurt me.

One day, she lost an enormous amount of money, so she grabbed me and pulled out the belt.

"If you guys don't tell me where the money is, your little sister is going to get a beating," my mother said.

"Please, Mom, don't hit Lupita!" my brothers said as I was crying.

She later found the money. My mother never really beat me that night, but the experience was traumatic, to say the least.

I always had a special love for my brother, being the only male figure growing up I felt protected by him. I remember one night coming from my Má Angelita's house, we always had to cross a major freeway to get home. That night was especially cold, so my mother wrapped me and herself with a shawl. I stepped on the shawl right in the middle of the interstate freeway, and we stumbled and fell in the middle of the freeway, unable to break free, as a truck was coming right toward us and it was too dark for the truck to see. My brother, being only thirteen years old, grabbed the shawl and, with his superhuman powers, managed to pull us to safety, with only seconds away from being hit by the truck.

All four of us hugged in tears. Ever since then, we have a special bond where no matter what we forgive each other, and we remained together.

Today, I could understand why she was so strict and bitter—after all, my father would often beat my mother. Violence was usual when my father visited, and we became abhorrent of him. But even he was not the monster I was afraid of.

Moving to the United States seemed the better option instead of staying and fearing having to live in front of the nightmare I once lived. The friendly and happy neighborhood I once lived in was no longer my happy place. The story of the bogeyman was all too real for me. Every time I went outside to play with my friends, I couldn't help but look on each corner of my eye every time I was left alone. I had no safety zone, I had no one to trust, and I wondered how and why it all just faded away. I feared my mother, I feared my father, and I feared every stranger on the street.

I remember looking out the window on our second floor and just gazing at the sky and asking myself, *Why are we here on earth and what is my purpose? Is there a better life than this?* I was a little girl at that time, but the experiences I had forced me into having a different outlook in life. Life is no longer games and dolls, little girl. There are bogeymen—adults with fears—and monsters out there, real monsters.

2

Journey

My last farewell with my two little friends, they invited me over. But I would often suggest we play outside instead, ever since that day. There are secrets best kept buried. Some secrets are too dark and incomprehensible that keep you searching for answers that you will never find. Since that day, I became a different little girl; I was robbed of my innocence. The days that followed were empty and no longer happy.

We had a toast by eating limes with salt from their backyard and sitting on their doorsteps. That was the last time I would spend time with them. I loved them, but I couldn't love them anymore.

We packed all our belongings in the small townhouse we owned in Mexico and headed to a better life, leaving everything we ever owned. But for both my siblings, they left relationships and friendships; I, on the other hand, was eager to leave it all behind. As a matter of fact, I was looking forward to leaving it behind and forgetting it all.

I didn't know that what we were embarking on was illegal. You just trust your parents—what child questions at that age? We traveled to Tijuana, Mexico, where we got into a bus that took us to a second location.

Inside the bus with other passengers, crossing the border in the middle of the night, I sensed the presence of fear in everyone as we approached our destiny.

"You can't take any belongings!" yelled the coyote.

"Just a small bag! You! You need to throw away those bananas!" he yelled at a young man carrying almost five pounds of bananas.

The young man carrying the bananas was a native Indian, and even I could tell he was clueless. There was a family of three with a little boy my age and three other men and one woman in the group. My sister the entire time was dreadfully quiet, and my brother kept giving us encouraging words. (As always, the cheerleader of the family.)

Adrenaline started rushing through my veins as I quickly realized what we were about to embark. I was sitting next to my mother and found myself hugging her with a tight grip. Still, I was determined to leave my past behind and start a new journey in this magnificent country.

We came to a stop inside the bus, and everyone seemed to be nervous as the bus stopping was a signal that we had reached the point of no return. The coyote again gave us instructions and made it clear that it was life or death, as he was pacing back and forth on the bus. He was in his twenties, fit, around five feet seven inches tall, and I saw he had a weapon on him and carried a small, black backpack.

"You do exactly as I say. When I say run, you run as fast as you can," the coyote instructed. "We will *not* come back for you." When I say shut up, you cannot even breathe. Any noise, and all of us will get caught. The water in the canal will be cold, and the stream might have rapids, you will need to continue to move through it."

It was dark, we came to a stop, and my heart kept pounding. The field looked empty, and you can sense everyone's fear. I was terrified of what was to come from the tension in the atmosphere.

We got off the bus, and it was pitch black outside. Most of us were not carrying anything, some had a small backpack, and others brought nothing at all. My heart was pounding, while others proceeded to climb the tall fence; I looked up at the fence and had no idea how I was going to climb over it. The grip on my hands got weak. It happens every time I get anxiety, a feature that I've always had but is completely useless.

I heard conversations of people being shot while climbing this fence. I knew we had to do this fast, as it was highly being observed by the Migra. I managed to climb the fence, and as soon as I did, we began to run on command; and we ran through for a few minutes. The terrain was hard to see, although I managed to see slight grass patches in the mainly deserted field.

The coyote kept directing us with just hand gestures. The family with the small boy my age kept holding us back, and I was completely annoyed by him. I really wanted to get to the other side. It had become apparent that I had a stronger character, yet I was still horrified of being caught.

We finally arrived at the canal; the water was filthy, muddy. We went in quietly. It was shallow, but the more we walked in, the colder and deeper it got. There was a section of rapids where I lost pace and started to drift from my mom and siblings. The rocks on the bottom of the river were slippery, and I was afraid of leeches or anything that lived in that canal, so I began to feel afraid and started whimpering.

I heard the boy crying, and just as I wanted to uncontrollably cry, the coyote told the family to shut their son up or they would need to be left behind. I buckled up, searching for my family. They were four to five yards away. I saw my brother going back for me then heard my mother tell him to leave me. At that moment, I started to panic. My breathing became heavy, and I started to have flashbacks as I heard my mother from a distance.

"No, you go. You must continue!" my mother said.

The terrifying event of crossing the canal and running for my life triggered memories of my tragic event when I was only five years old. Remembering two years back as I am, standing in the middle of the cold, dark canal, I was visiting my friend's house. It was early in the day, and we decided to play in her backyard since there was more traffic during the earlier times of the day than in the evening on our street. We started playing hide-and-seek.

Being the oldest, Karla went first. She started counting by one of the lemon trees as Erica and I ran to look for a place to hide in her house. The house had a lot of land with a shed next to the house. I ran after Erica, I lost her while running through the trees, and then I noticed the doors to the shed were opened. I assumed she went in, so I wandered inside the shed. I had never been in there before, but I could tell I was not supposed to be there by the machines inside, the rubble in one corner, and the metal and wood pieces lined up on a rack.

There was a cutting table near the second door that faced the street. I looked to hide behind the rubble, and just then, I saw a shadow of someone taller behind me on the concrete floor. I turned around and a male figure picked me up. My heart sank. I thought I was in trouble for going inside the shed. I knew he was young, possibly in his twenties, but I couldn't really take a good look between the kicking and fighting back. He tossed me on the cutting table and held me down. It was then when I knew he was going to hurt me, although I had no idea how. I was terrified as tears ran through my face.

I wore a yellow dress, ruffled underwear, and white ruffled socks with black shoes. I remember them so clearly because I kept looking forward toward the exit door, hoping someone would walk in. My house was just across the street, yet I thought I was never going to see my mother again or my brother and sister.

He began taking off my underwear, and he put his body weight on me to hold me down as he reached for my tiny leg. He pulled it up then started reaching for his pants and proceeded to do unspeakable things to me. I felt ashamed and dirty. I didn't comprehend what he was doing, but I knew it was shameful and dirty. I felt hopeless—I felt terrified.

Just then, I heard a laugh in the background. I looked behind and briefly saw Erica hiding behind the metal and wooden beams. He did not realize we were not alone and was alarmed by the laugh for a second. I took advantage of that second and ran out as fast as I could.

I felt betrayed by my friends, I felt ashamed, I felt dirty, I felt afraid. And since then, it was as if this giant shadow hovered over me, darkening my world and robbing me of my innocence. I didn't know who my assaulter was, and the not knowing who to be afraid of has always haunted me. When you don't know who to be afraid of, you are afraid of everyone that fits that profile. I went home that day and slept for the remainder of the day and the days that followed.

I didn't go out to play anymore. I was different since that day; I became quiet and timid. I stopped playing with dolls. It triggered memories as most dolls had ruffled socks and dresses back then. I began to have anxiety attacks, and that was where my indulgence in overeating began. Since that day—since that dreadful day—I wanted my father to take me with him. I wanted a new neighborhood. I wanted to forget that house with the shed and everyone in that town. Because only I knew the terrifying feeling I would get when I would wake up and go outside my home and see that house.

Back to crossing the border.

I caught up as they waited under a bridge in the canal. It was early in the morning, and it was cold. It didn't help that we were also soaking wet. I was shaking from anxiety from head to toe, and my jaw was clenched.

"As fast as you can, quietly move to the slope," the coyote barked his order.

We ran to a slope by the canal where he gave us instructions to remain extremely quiet until he said. I looked at everyone who was with us, and they were all terrified of what might happen next. The realization then hit me that if we moved, the Migra may possibly aim fire at us and my family might be shot dead.

We waited a few hours, and then came *La Migra*.

I could only hear the footsteps and see the flashing lights. Everyone got extremely quiet, hiding under bushes, camouflaged with mud. You couldn't hear them breathe. You could only sense the fear, dread, and absolute silence.

We waited for several hours until the Migra fell asleep in the patrol car.

The coyote ushered us to quietly go behind the patrol car across the highway. I saw the patrol car and two men sleeping inside. I feared them as if they were out to kill me. I was terrified of what could happen, had they woken up while we were still crossing. To me, they were the bad guys; to me, they were unreasonable and did not see us as human beings but as aliens—as if we were just a virus.

The suspense I was feeling at that moment while tiptoeing behind the patrol car was killing me, but you didn't have time to worry or act out your emotions. We crawled until we were far enough from the Migra.

"Vámonos, quick!" the coyote ordered. "Corran! Run!"

We ran from a slope across a highway where there was a vehicle.

3

The Promised Land

I must have slept for hours because my siblings woke me up, saying, "Wake up, we are here!"

I opened my eyes, and the first thing I saw was the big, neon 7-Eleven sign on Las Vegas Blvd. This was a clear indication that we had arrived to the United States as the sign was very foreign to me.

I had a sense of belonging, hope, and excitement on this new promised land—the land of dreams.

My father had already received amnesty through Reagan's 1986 Immigration Reform and Control Act. It was an amnesty that was a blessing to millions of people. Since the beginning, I fought to belong in this country. I wanted to learn and speak English right away. I wanted to be like everyone else who loved this country.

We arrived at our new house, which was huge compared to ours in Mexico. We spent the first days indoors, afraid to explore and leave the house. My siblings and I were arguing whether or not we should go to the store across the street. Something so normal all the sudden seemed so scary.

"What are we going to say at the store?" my brother said. "We don't speak any English."

"I know what!" I said.

"What, mensa, stupid?"

"Banana yogurt, it's the only thing I know how to say."

My brother and sister were laughing hysterically.

The first day of school was extremely scary for me. I didn't understand a word, and I felt like an outsider, like I obviously did not belong. I was listening to the teacher in the classroom and just heard rambling. I was completely clueless as to what was going on and afraid the teacher was going to punish me with a ruler like in my hometown.

We all wanted to fit in and belong. My brother wanted to belong and feel loved by my father. I could see it in his eyes the way he would try to impress my father. My brother always had the softest heart out of all of us; he was definitely outgoing and a social butterfly, the popular kid everyone just loved because of his kindness and humility. He had curly hair, perfect for the trendy hairstyles of the early nineties, so he would get the sides buzzed and wear one earring on his right ear.

My brother would often avoid the beatings from my mother because he had a way of melting my mother's heart by begging for mercy. I, on the other hand, would be quiet as a mouse during my beatings, showing no emotion whatsoever. This really bothered my mother, and eventually she wouldn't beat me anymore.

My father was always tired from work, short tempered, and often ignored all of us. He would binge-drink every night and on the weekends with his friends. While my brother was doing anything to be around my father, my father would just ignore him.

My brother quickly found acceptance in the wrong crowds. Twenty-Eighth Street was that wrong crowd (La Veinte-Ocho Gang). He began to dress in baggy pants with bandanas. He felt a sense of belonging once they gave him a nickname, Lambada. This was a thriving gang back in the late eighties to the early nineties that would require them to cause or commit violent crimes to be initiated into the gang. As a return, they promised to protect you and your family out on the streets from rivals. Unfortunately, this shed more blood out on the streets as rivals started to seek revenge with their own hands.

I would often see him sneak out in the middle of the night, only to come home drugged. My father only did what he knew best. He would beat him. The insults and beatings were so severe that it traumatized me by witnessing the violence my brother endured.

I thought he was going to die one time from a beating; my brother was on the floor curled in a fetal position while my father kept kicking him on the stomach and head until he started heavily bleeding. My mother was yelling from the top of her lungs.

"Stop! You are going to kill him!" my mother yelled.

My parents only argued even more. My father had chauvinistic beliefs, so my mother endured a rough marriage. My mother was raised without a father and had no idea what a normal marriage looked like. It doesn't help that our culture had the same old-fashioned chauvinism. (I am working on changing that.) Besides that, who were we going to call? My mother was so afraid to get any help because of our legal status. So we were defenseless.

I would often find my mother early in the morning crying, praying for my brother to return home. She wouldn't sleep all night, and she would then take the bus at six in the morning to work as a housekeeper in a motel, only to come back past six o'clock in the evening to cook for us and all my father's roommates who lived there as well.

Father had up to four other roommates in the house living with us. Although my father knew them, to me, they were perfect strangers. They all drank a lot and were very dirty. Most of them had family in Mexico or were single. My mother didn't sign up for this prior to coming here, neither any of us did. I always thought it was like in the movies: mother gets to stay home and father is always playful and happy coming back from work. But what does a hopeful child know?

I was observant, seeing everything for what it really was as if I was looking through a looking glass. Everyone was trying to survive in this alien territory, but nobody was trying to have a human connection. And we all desperately needed that emotional connection.

I saw brokenness, sadness and loneliness. At times I felt as if I were a ghost while everyone went on with their lives. My family would forget I was just a seven-year-old child in a foreign world. They would start their day without a care how I was getting to school, if I had lunch, or how homework was going or if we had any school fieldtrips. Who was going to care for me after school? Did I brush my teeth? These things were so insignificant yet so important but were forgotten. I was invisible to my siblings. After all, they had a tough time fitting in as well.

One day, it was two in the morning, and I heard footsteps. I woke up as my sister was exiting the sliding door. It worried me, but she had done that a few times before only this time she never came back. Perhaps, I was not the only one feeling the pain and stress of this new chaotic life.

Not only did my mother now have a son abusing drugs, an abusing husband, a harsh job that left her limbs in pain and exhaustion, but she now spends sleepless nights searching for her daughter endlessly, hoping she doesn't end up dead somewhere. The strength I saw in my mother was tremendous. Perhaps this was what helped me overcome my demons. Watching my mother have the strength to get up in the mornings and go to work and still manage to feed us in the evenings had always stuck with me. It was a type of strength only a mother can have. Mothers are so powerful, they harvest the power to create and to love unconditionally.

It took six months before we found out she had run away with my father's roommate. He was nine years older than my sister, and at that time, my sister was just turning eighteen years old. My parents took her back, but the roommate wanted to still live with my sister and eventually get married. My parents declined and told the man he can come for my sister once they got married. So they got married right away. My parents did not attend the wedding.

During the six months she was gone, I felt I no longer existed. My parents would get in the truck to search for her for hours every night. I would often walk into my mother's room and find her sobbing. Did they ever wonder how I was coping? It now crosses my mind.

I resorted to eating to fill my void in all those empty days. Something felt empty inside—the long hours of being alone lacking emotional support and love.

We eventually moved out to a bigger home.

I would spend my days playing on the new house we moved in. It was my father's boss's home, Mr. Moore. It was a couple of acres with a guest house in the back. That was the only thing that made me a cool kid at school.

I was put in an ESL class with the rest of the marginalized kids that had a second language. The ESL teacher was abusive, until finally one of the parents complained after the teacher had slammed a book on an Indonesian kid in my classroom.

Everyone avoided sitting next to me and often would talk about me. Because of my race and struggle to speak proper English, I was often bullied in school. I really didn't care because I could hardly understand what they said anyway. The bullying eventually got easier to handle as I got used to it. I was a chubby kid—or what my mother said, "thick boned"—had huge, long, curly hair; and my mother did not know if she had the time to take care of my kinky, curly ethnic hair. I didn't quite fit in with the Hispanic group because of my African features like thick lips and kinky hair, so I often made friends with African American kids or Asian kids.

I knew I had to take care of myself. My mother was often gone before I got up, so I would get myself ready at seven in the morning then walk alone to school and back. Oh, the day I broke a comb on my hair and couldn't get it out! I stayed home that day! Nobody had bothered teaching me basic hygiene like brushing your teeth, let alone caring for my coarse curls.

Often when I came home from school, my brother was already getting high in the house with his friends. So I never bothered him when I was hungry, scared, or needed help. I became independent and learned to take care of myself.

Because of all the freedom I had, I got to explore, build, and create. I built my tree house with my friend Lee. Lee was short and thin, with shiny straight, black hair and wore glasses, although he would often lose them. He was more fearful and restrained than me; I was always fearless and daring. But I guess I brought more excitement to his life, and he brought me company. He lived in the apartment next door, so we often played in my backyard instead. He wanted to become a doctor, so we often took in baby birds that had fallen from their nest. The baby birds would get better and eventually fly back to their home.

I grew up this way for a couple of years until my father started working as a bartender at The Mirage and would get great tips. My parents were able to buy a home on Sir Noble Street. The last night at my huge, old, miniature mansion, I sat on the front yard grass with Lee. I remember wearing a red shirt and jean shorts with a ponytail.

"Are you going to visit me sometime?" Lee asked me. "You should ask your mom and my mom if you can come over."

"Or maybe you can come over and I can show you my new home!" I told him.

"I have a secret," Lee said.

"What is it?"

"I can't tell you, you have to guess."

"Give me a hint."

"I like a girl."

My heart dropped to my stomach, and I felt uneasy.

"Who is it?" I asked him.

"She is wearing a red shirt."

That was the last time I saw Lee.

I made new friends, but I always remembered Lee.

4

Calm Before the Storm

That same summer after moving in, I broke my leg by climbing a tree, swinging from it with bedsheets. Ah, yes! That was not a great idea. But I had become a tomboy and daring. I would prefer riding my bike and doing tricks with it. I played with shopping carts by taking them to the top of the highest street then releasing it while you were inside it—another bad idea. If you ask me if I would allow my kids to do the same, I would blink my eye as I remember being tossed headfirst on the concrete and then slowly say, "Maybe if they wear a helmet."

My home seemed stable for a short period. I guess you can call it the calm before the storm. We went to Disneyland, and we vacationed in Mexico. Everything seemed all right for a short period. I even had a party for my tenth birthday. Happiness was never truly found ever since that dark event in my life, but I felt a sense of security just by my parents not physically fighting. Although my father has never really changed—he always had his narcissistic traits—I was content with no physical abuse.

My father was a swing-shift bartender and started abusing cocaine and alcohol more often. He began to get sloppy at work; he was late often and would show up to work high, so he eventually got fired. He was verbally more abusive and began to be physically abuse both my mother and brother. Everything began to fall apart in my home.

He would lock himself in the room for hours and was delusional. He was cruel and abusive to everyone—everyone but me. I remember he would just stare at my eyes, and I would stare right back as if he would find compassion in my eyes. I was so afraid in my own home, a fear that you can't seem to pinpoint. It was just a knowing that you were in fight-or-flight mode.

I began to hate my father. I hated how much pain he brought to my mother. I hated how cruel and evil he was. I hated how he treated my brother. I hated how cowardly he handled his friend taking my sister. I hated my father so much! But I never showed it. I internalized all my emotions, and it turned into an enormous frustration. I felt a frustration that I couldn't do anything about all the abuse. I harvested those emotions.

My mother was being more and more abused, and my brother eventually became an alcoholic with the continued fights for defending my mother. There was deep despair in my home. The chains of drugs, alcohol abuse, and domestic violence ran deep within my family; and I felt there was no way out of this lifestyle. It was a prison I desperately wanted to break free from.

I didn't want to accept that we came to this country full of opportunities—the land of dreams!—only for it to end like this. But the reality seemed far from a dreamland.

No happiness or peace ever came in those days, especially during the holidays when everyone is more cheerful and loving. My brother would tend to get into deep trouble, usually involving fights and jail. Mother always stayed up all night on Christmas as if she expected my brother to get into trouble. Every siren was her despair.

My brother came home sobbing like a baby one day, asking my mother for help, asking to go to a church so he can be prayed on by a priest. He hoped for a miracle as he realized he had become an alcoholic just like his father. But the doors were always closed when we arrived to the Catholic church. Out of despair, my brother sat on the front stairs of the church and just sobbed. In those days, all hope, all mercy had disappeared for our family.

My brother became my bully and I his scapegoat. I was an easy target to take out all his anger and frustration. I was often alone, but my father never abused me—at least, not physically. Seeing the difference in treatment, my brother would hit me, spit at me, and call me names. It was painful because I once was my brother's little sis and he would love me and pamper me, showing me around to his friends like a prized possession.

Those were the hell days—the days were long, and the months were endless. I wondered where the God that my grandmother often talked about was and why he abandoned me. Why was I not loved by God?

I avoided going to school; it was so stressful for me to go to school, on top of all the stress I had at home. I spent the days like a zombie, just going through the process. I couldn't wait to go home just so that I can be all alone in my thoughts.

At this time, my sister owned a home and had her first baby. My nephew was the only joy we had in our home, and he was the reason why my mother and sister started talking again. My sister lived only five minutes from our house, but my mom avoided asking her for help unless it was an emergency.

Unfortunately, we often had emergencies.

It was summertime, school was out, and mother was at work. She would leave me alone with my father, but he would often be out searching for more drugs. My brother had married and moved out of the house by then. He married his high school sweetheart. It was just me and my mother at that time, battling this huge, gigantic monster.

At midday on summer break, I got hungry—as a matter a fact, probably starving. By now, I was 12 years old; and being in the situation I was often in, I would go for days without eating. There was never any food in the house; as always, I assume my father would take the money for drugs instead of groceries. I picked up the phone to see if my sister was home, hoping she would pick me up instead of me walking five to six blocks in the 115-degree weather to her house. There was no phone service or cable.

I stepped outside to see if any of my friends were home, but I remembered that my friends had left a few days prior for their summer vacations. I looked right next door to my neighbor and noticed he was sitting on his lawn chair. I approached him. It was the easiest and fastest way to get a hold of my sister.

He was friendly and kindly said yes. I stepped inside his home, and he said, "The telephone is upstairs in my bedroom," as he pointed to the stairs. I didn't question why he had the only phone in his bedroom—after all, I knew he lived by himself.

I slowly walked up the stairs as I began to get an eerie feeling that something was off—he was right behind me. As soon as I saw the phone and entered his room, he locked his bedroom and threw me on his bed. He began assaulting me and pulling my pants down, a memory and feeling I knew all too well. I fought in anger and disbelief that was happening to me again.

His headboard was one of those nineties styles with mirrors and bookcases attached on the sides. I was searching for something to stab him with. I reached with my hand and grabbed pencils. Thankfully, one was sharpened well enough to get a good stab the first time. I just continued stabbing him; I wasn't looking where I was stabbing,

I had so much anger harvested from my previous sexual assault. He let go of me, and I fled. I ran out of his house and just kept walking fast toward my sister's house from the adrenaline of the entire experience. I didn't break down and cry; instead, I was afraid for my life.

Shortly after, there was a black Yukon truck following me. I noticed it was my neighbor's relative. He was trying to get me in the car, but instead, I started running faster. I knew that I couldn't let the man in the black SUV near me. They were afraid that I might run to the police and tell them what he attempted to do with me. It was not the assault they feared; they feared they might have opened Pandora's box. They had been drug dealing for quite some time, and they needed desperately to get rid of me as I was a nuisance now.

Since this event, I always looked at all corners of my eyes; I was constantly on alert for them. I feared one day they might get me. There was no way I was telling anyone or file a police report. I thought it would put me more in danger than I was already in.

Again, I didn't tell my family either, mainly because I knew they wouldn't care. If I had kept my previous assault a secret for so long, why tell anyone about this one? That was my reasoning. It was the reasoning of a twelve-year-old child living the life of a thirty-two-year-old adult that nobody cared for.

I always wondered what would have happened if I stopped to talk to the man in the SUV whenever I watched *Unsolved Mysteries*—

the stories of young girls gone missing and their bodies found in the desert or young girls forced into prostitution.

I became jaded and numb. I wanted out of the life I had been handed, and I wanted in someone's heart. I wanted to run, but I also wanted to be found. I wanted to be weak enough, fragile enough to be seen and rescued, but at the same time, I had so much anger that I wanted to fight. Was there a way out of this life? I felt a deep despair in my heart.

By the age of twelve, I already had experienced what most people will never experience in their lives, and yet I felt as if there was no compassion for my life. I was forced to be stronger beyond my natural capabilities at that age. I learned not to wait to be saved. I learned that the only one I can count on is myself and the only one who can protect me is myself.

Instead, I became tough; I dressed like a chola and hung around crowds so people could be scared of me. I wanted to know how to be tough. More than anything, I wanted to know how to be loved. I became someone that I really was not—a facade of a tough person when in reality I was sweet, shy, loving, and caring inside.

I wanted to be an FBI agent as a child so I can catch the bad guys. I liked reading, I wanted to play soccer, I was good at drawing and poetry, and I secretly loved school so much—I loved to learn. I saw the kids at my school who had a more normal life than me, and I yearned for a life like that. They seemed so happy and had smiles on their faces. But my life was far from normal. I was always scared of going home. I didn't know what new tragedy would happen or if we would need to flee from my father again. I was constantly in a fight-or-flight state.

I started smoking pot. I hated it so I only did it in front of certain people. If you want to fit in the gang, you need to blend in. Funny how this gang actually cared to listen and made you feel like you belonged.

I understand why now gangs are big and so easily appealing in the ghettos. The ghettos were filled with fatherless homes and mothers working long hours, too tired to give anything more to their children after they have already managed to push a warm plate of supper after a long day of work. As far as they know, they have given their all.

Giving emotional support becomes unrealistic to someone who is so broken and desperately needs it themselves. I saw that in my mother, but I desperately needed to feel love—I needed someone to talk to.

At one point I came home and my father was high as a kite, accusing my mother of infidelities that never happened, threatening to kill her while saying that the man having sex with her was right in our home hiding. He was completely delusional. There was no reasoning with him, and he was unpredictable. Seeing him in this state would trigger my PTSD from my previous sexual assault.

My stomach would feel as if I had knots in them, followed by a hot liquid that would spread weakness to my knees and hands. My palms would then become sweaty, and my heart rate would start to rise, which would be followed by a feeling of overwhelming fear and despair. I would then have moments where I constantly would replay my assaults over and over in my head. I would lock myself in my room and couldn't bear going to school during these episodes. I would walk to school, and halfway there, when I knew everyone was gone at home, I would turn back. I would be afraid to be around as other people and crowds gave me anxiety attacks. This went on for a long time.

I understand now that these were panic attacks and sometimes even PTD attacks from my sexual assaults.

Still in the situation I was in, I often had to take charge and save my mother from domestic abuse and potential harm. My mother would beg me to get help for her, not knowing of my own nightmares, not knowing how broken I had become. I looked at her eyes as they were filled with tears. I grabbed the phone and called the cops. My voice was trembling in fear while I caught my breath to talk to the police. I explained everything, yet they were reluctant to help us. That moment was how I realized how helpless we were.

It was terror in my home. No help came, and the feeling of helplessness just overshadowed my mother and me like a thick cloud—the night my father attempted to kill us.

My mother woke me up in the middle of the night crying, asking me for help. I remember specifically having so much anger toward her because at that moment I didn't understand why she couldn't find the courage to leave my father and never take him back. I thought my mother loved him so much more than me and that she was willing to die living with this man rather than protecting her children and leaving him. I didn't view my father as my father at that time. I viewed him as a terrible man. It is hard to describe the feelings I had for him at that time. I was tired, drained from the same thing, over and over again, so I pretty much told her to leave me alone. A few minutes later, my father walked in, chasing after her with a lighter, trying to put the house on fire.

We ended up leaving that night with no belongings. We spent the night at her friend's house. I realized we were homeless.

But she went back after we had nowhere else to go. Every time she went back, a piece of me died inside, hope died, love died; fear, hate, helplessness, unworthiness inhabited inside where love, stability, and wellness should have been; where dreams were made and love was born, where kids were safe, and where the foundation was solid. It all died; I was living in fear.

Things kept getting worse; my father looked ill, thin, and his face looked sunken. My father was bouncing checks and not paying the utilities by now. He was abusing drugs more and more now owing drug dealers. These drug dealers knew who I was out on the streets, and they would often harass me, making comments like "Maybe I should get my payment from you, sweetheart."

Until it happened. Oh, how I warned her!

5

Broken Pieces

My mother came back from work, and immediately it was noticeable that he was on drugs as always. But this time, he was highly delusional, and any move or sentence felt like you were taming a lion let lose in your home. He began assaulting her. I heard the screams in my room as she was begging for help. When I ran downstairs, my father had ripped off her clothes and was raping her. I couldn't do anything about it—I was frozen with fear.

I should have saved her; I should have done something, but I didn't—I was too weak. I grabbed the biggest piece of furniture and threw it downstairs to grab his attention. Anyone's attention!

Finally, help came. My youngest aunt and her husband came and witnessed the aftermath of my mother's disgrace as my father fled out of sight. My mother picked up her broken pieces and left that night. We left with very few belongings. We were homeless again for a few days. Because my father would stalk my mother and attempt to break in wherever she went, it was hard for anyone to take us in.

My father would show up at her work and cause a scene; he would show up at my sister's house and cause a huge scene as well. My sister's husband told us we had to leave. So we left again. We bounced around from home to home.

This might be why I have so much compassion for homeless people. Because I know how it feels to be in so much need and be rejected. I know how it feels to be unwanted, helpless, and poor.

My mother asked for a few months off work after finding out that she became pregnant; by now, she had started working at the

Treasure Island Hotel and Casino. Back then, they had amazing human resources. They gave her permission to leave, so we left for three months to our hometown in Mexico. It gave my mother time to think things through, and it gave her peace.

My brother took us in to his apartment afterward. We shared a two-bedroom apartment with his wife. He was also struggling with drugs and alcohol and domestic violence in his own home. Like father like son.

I avoided being around, so I would often leave, only to find the same garbage everywhere I went. I identified the baddest crew in the neighborhood, and I would make sure to befriend them in order to feel protected. It was a survival skill I had already learned by now. I grew up around drugs and alcohol, so it didn't scare me to see people I met also using this drug. I saw firsthand the destruction it caused to use drugs and alcohol, so I hated drugs and alcohol with all my being. Because I wasn't a druggie, it gave me an extra edge and made me the smartest in the group. I earned respect and avoided being humiliated like the rest of the girls who would get stoned and pass out at a perfect stranger's house.

I learned to carry a BB gun that reassembled a 9mm for protection. I don't know why I did it, honestly, could be that I was on edge all the time. Could be that I had PTSD. But I guess if you have been sexually assaulted twice by the time you are twelve years old, you would learn to do what it takes to protect yourself.

By this time I had the mindset of a thirty-year-old in a twelve-year-old's body that had developed too young. Thus, I looked way older than my age and would often get more attention from guys than I wanted, but I also got away with a lot more than I should. Because I looked older, I would often tell people I was sixteen as a form of protection to avoid making myself look vulnerable.

A wolf in sheep's clothing appeared in my life. He told me he was eighteen, and by then, I was already telling everyone I was sixteen. He was not eighteen; as a matter a fact, he was ten years older than me. And when I told him, I was twelve, he didn't seem to care. He treated me like a princess. I had never been shown so much attention and love in my life. He promised he would take care of me and started taking me out on dates alarmingly, with my mother's permission.

I desperately wanted to feel loved and cared for. I wanted to feel that I didn't have to worry at night because I had someone who loved me. So I fell for it like a little girl falls for free ice cream. I wonder if my mother hoped he could take me so she had one less thing to worry about. I didn't know her reasoning.

We eventually moved out of my brother's apartment and got an apartment, just around the corner from my sister's house. My world came tumbling down again.

My mother was seven months pregnant at that time, and my father had already slowly moved in with her. Again, we went back to the same. He would get drunk, drugged, and start assaulting her. Everything we worked for was gone, but this time, it was different. I was older and had become more independent and braver.

I confronted her, and I told her I didn't want my father living with us and she needed to have him move out. I did not want that life anymore, I didn't have the energy anymore, and I did not want my little brother to go through the hell I went through. She declined and said he was my father and couldn't force him out on the streets. I couldn't believe her words. I pulled all my strength from within and gathered courage to tell her what happened to me.

I told my mother, "Do you realize that while you left me with my father, he went out to get drugged and my neighbor sexually assaulted me?"

She told me I was a liar, and as soon as I heard those few words, I felt stabbed in the heart.

"You just want attention!" she continued.

My world came crumbling down, and the very last bits of trust and feeling of safety I ever had with her were shattered. At that moment, I realized I had been unloved for so long; at that moment, I felt so alone and so unworthy of anything and everything. My mother at that time was my only lifeline, my only safety and security. When she said those words to me, it changed me. I went back and recounted on all my experiences in my life, and when I recounted all those events, I realized how many times I was left to deal with my own emotions and fears.

Gosh, does God even love me? How can he? I asked.

My mother had become incapable of giving love. She was too broken to raise me. The real question is, Since when and for how much longer?

I slipped into a huge abyss of depression. I began having nightmares, and then I realized that I no longer wanted to live. I came to the conclusion that no one would miss me. I decided that day that I would take my own life. The pain of living was greater than the thought of continuing to live in my world. My bottom fell out, I felt empty and exhausted from my emotions, and the power that I had to gather to continue living in my own shoes was gone. I had no purpose. I had no one to love me, and I had no one to love.

I drank the entire bottle of Tylenol, hoping that would do the trick, and then I just waited.

Instead, my temperature dropped, my hands became sweaty, and my skin turned pale. I was too weak to move, but my heart was racing. I was ready for death, but subconsciously I was screaming for help. Does anyone care? Can someone come find me? My deep subconsciousness said as if it was my soul that needed rescuing and not my body.

My mother found me in my room sick and asked me several times, "What is wrong with you?" She found the empty bottle of Tylenol and immediately took me to her doctor.

Rather than pumping the medicine out of my system, the doctor decided it would teach me a lesson to not ever do this again by having me endure the pain. No questions were asked what was going on in my life that made me actually attempt to kill myself.

Again, there was no hope or help for the helpless. But there were many signs I gave, many whispers and soft voices that if any mother just paid attention, they would hear the cry of the child, begging for help, begging for love. The times I was too quiet, the times my mother thought of going in my room but then went on to do something else, the times I came back from school for the hundredth time with a D- and instead of asking what was truly going on—she just brushed it off with "maybe the kid is not smart," "maybe the kid is just bad," "maybe the kid is irresponsible," or "maybe the kid is promiscuous."

My suicide attempt was not a whisper; it was a scream for help. It was "Help, I'm dying in real life, and I desperately need you! Because

I've been hanging on to too much and am just a baby, I can't carry the weight of it all anymore! And I can't carry the weight of your problems anymore when you should be carrying mine!"

But no one heard my scream because my mother was too broken to hear my pain. She was exhausted, broken, and needed rescue, just like me.

It seemed that the only escape was to runaway but to whom? I had no one.

I was mad at the world, let down by the system, my parents, my family, my doctor. I developed bulimia around this time. This condition lasted over a decade. It wasn't to be skinny—although the consequences of this condition helped with being thin—it was a compulsion to eat and fill a void I felt, but I would feel so sick to my stomach and would have awful pains.

I eventually made a friend. This friend helped me feel like I had someone who cared for me. We laughed so hard at times, and she too was having struggles of her own so we found support in each other.

I was getting on the bus when I met her, and I remember I immediately clicked with this chick. She was funny while wearing a blue NFL shirt with matching eye shadow. I felt like home with her, and we became best friends. This school was full of gangs, and they would really get violent, so you either joined them or you got out of their way and stayed low. Like Angie used to say, "I'm a lover, not a fighter, however I always seemed to attract trouble." I had my own rules and thought I could be friends with rival gangs if I wanted.

I started fighting at school; I didn't care if you were six feet tall and three hundred pounds like Tamika, my classmate who made a simple comment insulting my religious preference. My faith in Jesus was the only thing I truly believed in; faith was the only thing I had control over, and even then, it seemed to slip at times.

Tamika was gothic and hated me for no discernable reason. So I told her, "Let's settle this after school," and I did. Walking across the street, she pushed me from behind; and before I knew it, I had a 300-pound mass of body on top of my 110-pound body pounding on me. Tamika kept landing punches at me, and I knew that if I was going to fight her, I needed to be smarter than her since she was 3 times my weight.

I grabbed her by the hair and put my entire weight on her until she made it to the ground while I twisted one arm and I kept pounding at her face. I don't remember how or when it ended. I just remember fighting until everyone started running from the cops. I thought she had really done a number on me. The next day, her parents had filed a report and informed my mother that I had sent her to the hospital.

I am not proud of this; I just had so much anger and wanted to fight.

6

Epiphany

I met a woman named Maria when I was invited to ditch school and go party at her house instead. Maria was known as the motherly chola of Twenty-Eighth Street. She threw parties for the Twenty-Eighth Street kids at my junior high school. She was fun and seemed to care for me, so I opened up about my family problems.

She told me I could come live with her; so without hesitation, I went home, I waited for everyone to leave the house, and then I quickly grabbed two black trash bags and threw in as much as I could in there and left. I was hoping to not ever come back.

The first night there, I was officially jumped in to the Twenty-Eighth Street Gang.

My brother seemed to be some sort of legend to them, so I was respected by everyone. I felt empowered and cool for a twelve-year-old kid with no parenting and rules. We all think that it is cool to not have any parenting, but the truth is that we don't. We want loving, caring parents who listened to us—really listened to us—and cared about what we had to say. We all wanted the annoying parent who asked about our day and wanted to hear about our friends and kept asking us how school was going and if we needed help with anything else. I craved parenting because it meant that someone loved and cared for me and that it's a sign of security and a sign that I am not alone. All kids want parenting, no matter what they tell you.

With the gang, every night was a party. Every night the boys brought in so much weed in the house and smoked until they passed out. But Maria had two young daughters and often she would neglect them, and it would break my heart to see them get neglected so I became the older sister and started caring for them. Everything became all too familiar, and then I realized the gang was no different than what I had left.

A few weeks later, word soon spread that I had been on the news and my mother was looking for me. Not long after that, a private detective came in to Maria's house to search the house. She hid me in a basket of clothes inside a closet until they were gone. It became apparent that I needed to go home.

I had a different perspective when I returned. I had tasted independency and knew that I had one goal—to break the chains of abuse and drugs of this life into which I was brought.

My little brother was born in November; he was beautiful and perfect. I took care of this little guy as much as I could. By then, the man dressed in sheep's clothing returned. He lied to me as well. He never loved me and he was never going to care for me. He had one goal—abuse and use me just like everyone else. He didn't care that I was a minor child; he just saw the opportunity to take advantage.

It seemed all four walls kept closing in on me, with no escape from the life I was so sick of. I believed in him because what else did I have to believe in? He caused a wound so deep in my heart that I can still hear my soul cry from it. He took the last bit of hope I had and threw me in to an abyss deeper than ever before. Men can do that when you fall in love, except I was not in love with him. I just wanted stability and love.

As soon as he found out I was pregnant, he left.

7

Crossing Over

I remember walking in to class with morning sickness; it was just all too apparent that I was pregnant. Feeling alone and degraded, it made those long halls in school so dark and cold. My future—if I had any—was completely wiped out, as if I had a blank book in front of me. I didn't know where I was going to end up.

It was second period, just six minutes until the bell rang. I was counting every second, until finally I ran out of the classroom, down the hall, straight to the girls' bathroom, barely making it to the toilet. I had horrible morning sickness, and I stayed in the bathroom and quietly sobbed. As the bell rang, the girls walked in. Hearing their normal teen conversations and gossip made me realize how different my world had been and how much more it was about to change. I just stood in the stall until they were all gone. A lot was running through my mind at that moment, mainly the thought *What if I'm pregnant?*

My room was dark quiet when I got home. I took advantage before my mother got home and took the pregnancy test. Two lines read the pregnancy test for a positive, yet I had so many negatives against me. Somehow, I felt an enormous amount of peace and love at that moment for the life that I was bringing forth.

It was at this moment when I decided that I could not possibly make the same mistakes that my family made!

I made the decision of crossing over!

I decided to break the generational chains of oppression and the mentality that this is how it is supposed to be.

I didn't know God at that pivotal moment in my life, but he knew me and he knew my heart.

When my mother found out I was pregnant, she immediately pulled me out of school and started making arrangements for an abortion or a boarding school in Reno, Nevada. My family was embarrassed by my situation. I was in the seventh grade at that time. I often wonder now that I'm older and have two daughters what her expectation was after knowing this man was ten years older than me.

I refused the abortion. My whole life I had never been loved, and now they are planning to take the only one that I can unconditionally love? I refused to have the abortion.

My sister told my mother that she needed to discipline me by forcing me to figure everything out on my own. I was immune to cruelty already. Frankly, I didn't care. When had anyone ever done anything for me? Her rationality made no sense to someone who had been through hell already and back without being noticed. But I knew that my sister was bitter because she was forced into a marriage that she was unsure of and my parents never showed up to her wedding. They never spoke to each other until my nephew was born.

This was a blessing in disguise.

8

Viridity of Motherhood

The next few months, while my still very young body was growing a baby, I spent my days contemplating who God was as he was calling me closer. It would be a couple more years before I would accept the Lord, but he was already working—he was already guiding me and protecting me in so many ways.

It only takes one strong-willed person to take the first step to break that generational curse; and with the power of Jesus Christ, your family can be healed through persistence in prayer, faith, forgiveness, and unconditional love. I knew I had to fight to make this happen, and it didn't matter how difficult or impossible it was because what mattered was that you just keep pushing forward, no matter where you start or how you start.

My journey started with asking for help.

I found myself at the welfare office filling out applications and signing my mother's name as the adult because she was unavailable and couldn't fill out any paperwork. I took the bus to get around. I went to the DMV on my own to get identification. I then went to the welfare office to apply for Medicaid. I would fill out applications and then ask for my mother's social security and paystubs because she was the adult in my care. I was thirteen years old at that time, and because my mother worked and my sister did not want to help me, I did this all on my own. I set up all my medical care and even found charities that could also help my mother with my little brother.

Figuring everything out on my own has taught me so many invaluable lessons in life because now there is nothing I can't figure out on my own. This was the blessing in disguise.

My mother couldn't afford a babysitter for my brother and had me care for my brother. I learned through the care of my little brother how to care for a baby. In my viridity of motherhood, it's easy to immediately learn once you understand the unconditional love of being a mother, no matter your age.

Having to be on my own, figuring things out in this big world, and wearing the shoes of an adult took my mind off a lot of things; it gave me something to look forward to. It gave me motivation. It forced me to fight; after all, fighting is all I know. All the pain I harvested was now being redirected to bettering myself; it was redirected to love.

I found a teen pregnancy clinic. I was so grateful that there was a place where you can literally find all the resources you needed. They tested me for pregnancy; upon getting a positive, they gave me a bunch of free vitamins and free items. I felt a sense of relief and hope that there was help for someone like me.

I had to take the bus to my visits back and forth, well into my last trimester. My last trimester was the hardest. I was often left with no money to take the bus, so in mid-July, I would walk five miles to the clinic near UMC Hospital. The obstetrician put me at high risk so they would see me every one to two weeks. I would often find myself crying throughout my pregnancy. But when you are given lemons, you can't sit there and cry all the time. Eventually you get thirsty and make lemonade.

When the baby shower was fast approaching, expecting, celebrating, and planning for a child are all too exciting! For me, I just couldn't wait to see my little one's face, to hold him, and love him. I had everything perfectly planned and ready for him, and every little gift or item would just add more excitement.

My mother and sister planned for a baby shower, and honestly, I was excited. I had no friends at the time; I stopped contact with everyone, just to keep away from bad influence, and my good friends were asked to stay away from me because I was the bad influence (ironically). So I was counting on my mother's friends and my sister's friends.

No one showed up.

I sat just holding my head up and forcing a smile, only I think I never really smiled as my frown kept fighting my fake smile. It was apparent that it was me. Every event that my sister ever had was a packed house but not for me—as if I and my newborn were an embarrassment to everyone.

A week later as I was mopping the floor, I slipped and fell. That night, I began with labor pains. Eventually, my mother woke up, noticing that I kept moving every five minutes. My mother was the only person at the hospital with me. I didn't expect anyone; I wasn't looking forward to flowers after giving birth. My son was born August 5, 1996, naturally with no anesthesia, at just thirty-seven weeks, weighing five pounds and eleven ounces. I had just turned fourteen years old one month prior.

9
Just the Two of Us

I took my baby in my arms and gazed at him for so long. He was the most beautiful person I had ever seen. He gripped my finger with his tiny hand. He was full of innocence and love. He was my reason to fight, I thought to myself, as I looked at his pink face with angelic features. I promised him I would always be there for him and would always protect him from harm.

I breastfed my child and did everything an adult mother would do the best I could. Mexican moms have so many rules: "Wear a sweater!" or "Cover yourself up!" or "Drink lots of avena (oatmeal with milk drink)!" Every Mexican mom would say, "You have to sweat for the milk to come down!" Somehow, I felt as if my sister felt resentment and would sabotage me. I never understood why my sister hated me so much. I understand now that these times were difficult on all of us.

I would often go to the Catholic charity to get diapers and items, sometimes for both my little brother and son. WIC and other Catholic charities were my best friends! They got me out of a pickle most times.

While my friends were busy going to the movies or to the high school games and hanging out with friends, I was busy raising my little boy. I got my first job at the age of fourteen, shortly after my son was born. I was a receptionist at my brother's in-laws' business. It did not last very long, but it made me realize that I needed good income to support my child. I started desperately wanting to go back to school because now I had hope and motive. My son was my world and the only one I had—I wanted to give him the best.

My grandmother came to visit us for a few months after hearing all the rumors that my father had become a drug addict and was living on the streets at times. She couldn't bear to believe such a thing—after all, what mother would believe horrific news of their own child? At that time, she was staying at my aunt's house, and as I was so close to her, I would come visit her as much as I could.

My mother and I ended up moving out of my sister's house. We got tired of the animosity, plus her husband kicked us out. We ended up moving to one of the worst places in town, mainly because we needed to do a fast move. Again, we found ourselves starting over.

Moving had become common.

My grandmother cared for me so much! I questioned why sometimes, and I also question if she treated everyone else the same. She often said that it was because I always spoke truth and honesty. I am actually proud of that, and that is something I take to my heart from her.

It would take almost two hours to go visit her and sometimes longer. She hated that I had to go through so much trouble to come see her, so she got her neighbor to lend me a car. I am still shocked that he agreed after all these years; I mean, who in the world would do such a thing? Lending a car to an old lady's fourteen-year-old granddaughter?

He did, and in less than five minutes, I had to learn how to drive. I'm not going to lie—I was nervous as heck, and I have no idea how I managed to drive and what got in my mind to endanger my child. But I didn't see danger like normal people did. The way I was raised, I had a completely different perspective than I do now.

Nevertheless, I was scared of one thing—my mother.

I would park the car on the street behind ours and walk to the mobile home. I did this for about three weeks. As soon as my mother left to work, I would go places. I was able to locate my son's father. I wish I never did. I wish I could have saved myself the humiliation of confronting that heartless man. He and his family were foul, and I knew my son didn't deserve to be around them. But at least it brought closure, and to this day, I am grateful I kept my son away from them.

Until, my grandma's neighbor called our house several times asking for Lupita. My mother finally said, "Well, my name is Lupita, but I don't know you and I don't know what the heck you want!"

"Lupita, please I beg you to not act dumb. I need my car back," the neighbor said.

"I have no idea what you are talking about!" my mother replied.

"You don't remember? Your grandma asked me to lend you my car?"

My mother gave me that look, the look she gave me plenty of times right before I got a good beating. I felt my tonsils drop to my stomach. We left that same night to drop off the car to this poor man.

Summer was soon ending, and I just couldn't wait until I was old enough to work so I can support my son. As soon as I was old enough, I got hired as a telemarketer for a mortgage company. I was good at pretending, and all the times that I made phone calls for my mother helped me out. They gave us the minimum hourly wage plus twenty dollars per appointment. I thought it was the best job in the world. I loved the atmosphere of so much success happening around me!

I still believe I was the only excited person working there. It was the first time that I was ever exposed to successful folks with money. I sometimes was able to set four to six appointments a week, which gave me an extra hundred dollars a week on top of my salary. That was a lot of money back in 1998 for a first job.

I wanted to know what it takes to be at their level. So one day, I sat on the desk next to the window so I can see when the brokers came in to pick up their appointment sheets. And there he was, walking in, wearing a Giorgio Armani suit with a Rolex and a leather briefcase. His shoes were shiny, and his perfume smelled sweet like money.

I stood up and took the opportunity to hand him my appointment sheet personally, and I asked him, "What do I need to do to get to your level?"

He looked straight at me and said, "Sweetheart, you first need to finish high school!"

He was right! He was absolutely right! But if that's the first step, consider it done! For the first time, I found sense in going back to school. I now not only had motivation, but that event had lit a fire in me to succeed and do whatever it takes to get to his level.

I quit that summer and enrolled to Clark County High School, hoping to put my child in the day care that the school provided. But the waiting list was long, about two to three months long. I enrolled anyway, thinking to myself that God will make a way for me to finish high school.

The halls were full of kids acting like kids. I looked at them, and I wondered how it would feel like, what it would be like. How does it feel for the high school gossip to be the most important thing in the world? Meanwhile, I had to make money to afford for a babysitter during the day, so I applied everywhere and anywhere where they were hiring for afternoon shifts so that I can attend school during the day.

I would take the bus after school and applied at various jobs. I didn't wait for a call back; I would show up and ask if they received my application, hoping for an interview at that moment. One of the managers at McDonald's referred me to another location across town, so I took the position. I didn't make excuses at that moment, for I had one goal and one desire that nobody was going to take away. I had nothing to lose and no one to count on but myself.

I was already at the very bottom of the scale and had nowhere else to go but up. To me, it didn't matter where I started as long as it kept me on track of my goal! I had a burning desire for a better life! I needed a better life like I needed air. I needed my son to have a different life than the one I had.

In 1997, the song "Just the two of us" by Will Smith came out, and it reminds me so much of me and my son and everything that we had to go through. My little guy and I were doing the best we can against the world and against all odds. Times got difficult, but when I looked at my little guy's eyes, it made it all better. I don't know who raised who. My little guy made me grow into a mother and woman, and he gave me strength when I needed it.

10

Determination

I began working during the evenings and went to school during the day. It was hard, I was tired and sleepy during the day, and I would try very hard not to sleep during class. I would check in every other day at the school day care, hoping there was room for my son so that I didn't have to work evenings. I would take the bus across town to this high school at six in the morning and carried my work uniform in my school backpack so I can go straight to work afterward. This is how I met my ex-husband.

I had seen him six months back while briefly stopping in and just thought how cute he was. Little did I know I would get to meet him. He was my supervisor and had a hilarious humor. We had instantly gotten along when we first met. He noticed I would take the bus home late at night, so he offered to take me home. Then one day, while putting away a delivery, he swept me up in his arms and kissed me. We dated a few months.

I was exhausted but driven to have a better life. I worked and went to school as long as I possibly could. My mother couldn't worry about who would take care of my little brother or my son. I had to pay and figure it out many times.

At one point, I had nobody to care for my little ones, so I asked one of my neighbors. I noticed she was always home and figured since she was two doors down, I can literally just walk them to her house every day. She didn't speak any English but was a very kind older lady. She was kind enough to have her son-in-law give me a ride to work one day, and for what it was worth, that was the only day I was given a ride from them.

I had come to her house the day they gave me a ride to work to let her know I was going to work. I could see my house from hers, and she grabbed her purse and walked toward my home then asked, "Do you need a ride, honey?" I said, "That would be so nice of you." At that point, she went back to get her son-in-law, and out he came so willingly to do me a favor. I got in the car and waved at her as she was standing right outside my house.

A few hours later, a cop came to my work asking for me. I didn't have a clue; my boyfriend saw the cop detaining me, and it was one of the most embarrassing moments in my life! I was not read my Miranda rights at all; he simply handcuffed me and took me to juvenile jail. The officer didn't have a clue of the crime I had committed, but somehow, they managed to put me in jail. Being asked to get undressed so they can thoroughly search me was the most degrading and humiliating part of the process, not to mention that I didn't even know what I had done.

When they finally questioned me, I realized that the babysitter had accidently locked the kids in my home; then instead of calling me, she called the neighbor for help. But with her broken English, the neighbor thought the kids were left by themselves then proceeded to call the cops. My two boys were put at Child Protective Services.

My mother eventually came home then picked me up, as well as my little brother and son. I thought my boyfriend was never going to talk to me again. I don't know what crossed his mind, perhaps he saw the need to be there for me.

One night, he was asked to switch a shift with Cliff the store manager, and he agreed with the condition that Cliff would take me home. That night changed everyone's life forever. I had no idea that a simple decision can change the course of destiny—something that my ex-husband still thinks about 'til today

I was scheduled to close the restaurant that night with Luis, Robert, and Cliff. Luis was Hispanic, thin, tall, and spoke very good English and lived with his father and two sisters attending UNLV. Robert aspired to be a professional football player and was very talented. Cliff was a very tall black man weighing well over

250 pounds. He had several children and had so many people who loved him because of his magnetic personality. He was also very good friends with my ex-husband.

That night, after closing, Cliff offered to give everyone a ride home. I lived so far away, but he wanted to get me home first. We were headed down Charleston Boulevard, and I was sitting on the passenger seat, with Robert directly behind me and Luis behind Cliff. I briefly saw a Greyhound bus moving toward the intersection, and we were traveling on a green light. The greyhound continued even though it saw us. Cliff hit the brakes, the car swerved to the left, and the Greyhound bus hit my side of the vehicle head-on.

The car spun out of control, making a few spins several times, until it finally came to a stop. I lost consciousness for a few minutes. When I came back, I immediately thought of my son. I am all he's got was my first instinct to survive out of this. The impact hit my head, causing a deep cut and broken pelvis, knee, elbow, and wrist, as well as ruptured spleen and neck ligaments with moved spine disks.

When I came back from consciousness, I saw a man asking, "Are you okay? Oh my god! Are you okay?"

I couldn't talk much. I looked up at Cliff on the driver's seat, and part of his nose and upper lip were missing. His head had smacked the rear-view mirror, and it tore his flesh off. His entire upper body had collided with the steering wheel, and at that moment, I saw that he was dying as his body was bleeding out from his internal organs now exposed on the steering wheel.

He looked at me, and his final words were "Hang in there."

I saw the paramedics arriving, but by the time they got to Cliff, he was already gone.

I then heard Robert crying, "I can't breathe." They took him out onto the stretcher. The paramedics couldn't get me out of the car as the car had crashed head-on on my side of the vehicle. I patiently waited as I too was bleeding internally; the adrenaline rush had kept my body from not feeling pain. They began to jigsaw the car to get me out, and then I noticed I had not heard Luis.

Stuttering I asked the paramedics where Luis was, and with a surprised response, the paramedic asked, "Is there someone else in here?" I said yes.

The paramedic searched and saw body parts underneath Cliff's seat. The impact had crushed him underneath the driver seat. The despair I heard in their voice as they were pulling him out has made me love and respect them for their service so much.

Luis was put in ICU and unplugged from life support a month later.

Cliff died that night.

Robert had a long recovery as he needed emergency surgery.

I was in ICU from internal bleeding and a head injury, but most of my injuries were from fractured body parts. They eventually transferred me to a rehabilitation center so I could learn how to walk again. The place was depressing, cold, and isolated. I became depressed and refused to eat. All my previous experiences came back, all the previous pain all of the memories and feelings attached to them were back. I was finally at a good place in my life prior to this accident; I had finally found the drive I needed, and now this happened.

How many times can my spirit be punched down before I finally give up? I was beat and tired, physically, mentally, emotionally, and spiritually.

Since the day of the accident, my ex-husband stood by my side every single day. But I missed my son; he didn't understand why I was gone or what happened to me. I begged my mother to bring him to visit. She was reluctant because she didn't know how he would react or how it would affect him. I was wearing a neck brace, had a cast on my leg and wrist, and couldn't walk.

The nurses wheeled me to meet my son at the entrance. When I saw my son walk through the doors of the rehabilitation center, my heart was so full of joy again. He saw me and had the most worried look on his face. He looked up at the nurse and kicked her. My poor little boy probably thought the nurses there were hurting me.

I went deep into depression. How much hurt can the heart take before it ceases to exist? How much tragedy and disappointment can someone go through before it simply gives up in life? I asked myself this question over and over again and was just frustrated at the fact that I knew that I could—and I should—have a better life than this. But I just didn't understand why I was going through this at that time.

I questioned God again, *Why?* But it was not the right timing yet for God to answer my questions. You have to be ready to receive in order to hear the truth.

I eventually got well enough to go home with a walker and wheelchair. I was told that the fracture on my pelvis might have injured me well enough that I might never be able to have children again. The trauma of seeing my friends die, on top of my injuries, took a while to recover.

The battle with Greyhound Lines attorneys began, and I truly think some attorneys have no soul in order to represent companies with huge pockets. The intimidation and the way they would make me look and feel was degrading to say the least. They were trying to make me seem like a peasant so that the compensation was minimal. I knew I was better than what they had me as. I knew I was not a nobody; I knew that I was not going to remain living in the ghetto with no future. I knew then I was not going to become what they had me as—a mediocre teen mom who would never account for anything in life, just hoping to get some cash from this prestigious company. I refused to live by their title!

The attorneys had one thing right—I had all odds against me. I had almost every possible tragedy and disadvantage in my life. But they had no idea what the power of will and faith could do.

I was tired of being marginalized, stereotyped, stigmatized, discriminated, and misjudged in this country. I failed to believe and accept that in my life. I was determined to not become another statistic. I didn't need to prove anyone anything! I needed to prove to myself that I could become successful in this country and that liberty and justice could be obtainable. Because after all, no matter what the interpretations are of our Pledge of Allegiance, the direct meaning is liberty and justice for all.

We all have the liberty to demand the same rights as others—to achieve the same level of success, to apply for the same jobs as others, to attend school and not be denied of the same basic needs as others, and to work hard and be promoted with my race, color, or ethnicity not being a subject in the matter of justice being served. It is only when you realize how important having those rights truly are that you take advantage of the right to be able to exercise them and to live in this country under the same flag as everyone else.

11
Reflections

After my car accident, I had multiple therapy appointments for a week and had to be cared for like a child. My dreams of finishing high school had seemed to be shattered at that time. Perhaps it was my time to heal, my time to mourn, and my time to gather my broken pieces. Healing takes time. It is a process that cannot be bargained with and cannot be bought. Both in the physical world and in the spiritual realm, healing is a natural process.

There is a passage in the Bible that reminds me of this stage in my life:

> A Time for Everything
>
> There is a time for everything,
> and a season for every activity under the heavens:
> a time to be born and a time to die, a time to plant and a time to uproot,
> a time to kill and a time to heal,
> a time to tear down and a time to build,
> a time to weep and a time to laugh, a time to mourn and a time to dance,
> a time to scatter stones and a time to gather them,
> a time to embrace and a time to refrain from embracing,
> a time to search and a time to give up,
> a time to keep and a time to throw away,
> a time to tear and a time to mend,

a time to be silent and a time to speak,
a time to love and a time to hate, a time for war and a time for peace. (Eccles. 3:1–8)

Every season has a lesson so pay attention to what it's trying to teach you.

This part of my life became my journey to discover myself and to become more spiritually aligned with God. I started going to a Christian church. It was my way of healing my broken spirit. I accepted the Lord in Alcanse Victoria that summer after I came back from the rehabilitation center. A seed of faith was planted in me, and that day, I accepted the Lord. And it made me thirst for more of God's word.

My boyfriend and I continued dating through this journey of mine, and in October 1999, I became pregnant. But immediately, he avoided telling his parents about my pregnancy.

At first, I didn't realize that he was avoiding taking me to his parents' house; but after time, it was apparent that he didn't want me around his family. He never told his parents I was pregnant, and after seven months of pregnancy, my mother got very upset and simply picked up the phone and told my ex-husband's mother that I was expecting and would give birth any day now.

My mother-in-law was shocked, to say the least. My in-laws had warned my boyfriend that he needed to end our relationship because it would never work out. I had baggage (a son), and that was their reasoning. From the start, I felt off and unaccepted by his parents and his family. In return, this made me distance myself even more from his family. I knew that relationship was never going to work, but even then, I was hopeful. The coldness and differential treatment continued for many years, but I had no time to deal with that issue at hand. I had a bigger problem.

My daughter was born with a severe urinary tract reflux on both ureters. At just 30 days old, she had a severe 105-degree fever, started having seizures, and went into shock. I thought she was going to die at that moment as I was holding her in my arms; my little brother at that time was four and a half years old and asked me if she was going to die. I looked up to God and begged him to not take my daughter.

We rushed her to the ER and immediately got taken back. The nurses started working on her and escorted me to the quiet room. That was the beginning of a very long battle with her illness and countless days with her admitted in the hospital. I remained a rock during my daughter's sickness, but it was when we couldn't find one good vein on her anymore when I lost it and started crying uncontrollably. All her veins were no longer good from being poked so many times, and the nurses couldn't find a good vein. When the RN finally came in and informed me that they might have to shave her head was when I lost it. She had gorgeous curly hair.

My daughter eventually had surgery at the age of two years old that lasted nine hours. Those nine long hours of her being in surgery were unbearable. There were so many things that could go wrong. I paced back and forth, from one room to the other. It's hard to say this as a mother, but then I heard it from my own mother's voice—"A mother doesn't love her child more than the other but instead is there for the child that needs her at that moment." I was there for my daughter, and now I recount on my oldest son and realize that I unfortunately had to leave him in the care of family members so many nights and so many times. A mother always wishes to split herself and be there for everyone. And so again, my son was parentless while I was in the hospital.

The holidays were the hardest for me. It was December 23, 2002—just a few days from Christmas—and we had already made the hospital our home for the past three and a half weeks. I was really hoping for my daughter to get discharged from the hospital so I could surprise my son for Christmas. Dr. Ganesan was her surgeon. He came in her room and asked how she was doing and said, "If her urinary test comes back clean, you can go home tonight."

We waited anxiously, and finally, her results came back clean. I was excited to go home, so I called my husband right away. I grabbed the phone with excitement to tell him that we were coming home, but there was no answer, so I left a message. I waited but no answer. I kept calling for the next two hours while I was packing one month's worth of belongings that had accumulated there at the hospital, but still no answer.

I was furious by now! Doesn't he know he has a sick child in the hospital? How could he not care? I had been taking all the load of caring for my daughter and sleeping every day on a rocking chair and waking up every two hours, sometimes having sleepless nights. He never picked up. I left that night alone.

My daughter was delicate; she still had the catheter tube to drain her bladder placed through her lower abdomen instead of the vagina. When I arrived, I called him again, and he finally answered. I was furious and yelled at him. He came downstairs to the parking lot and started hitting me in front of my daughter. I screamed for help in the parking lot, but it was late at night and the parking lot was empty. I stayed with him regardless because I didn't know what else to do. I was drained emotionally and physically after being there night and day for my daughter, and I also wanted to make Christmas the best possible for my son and daughter.

Through that time, my husband was physically abusive, emotionally disconnected and aloof, and would often drink and gamble. There was never any romance in our relationship or marriage. Everything that could go wrong with a marriage went wrong. He was not ready to settle, and with his side of the family making things even harder, it was evident he was not going to change.

I have no excuse why I didn't leave him at that moment. I can only tell you that when you don't know what love looks like, you just don't know.

My father always abused my mother, and she never left. I was sexually abused twice, and depending on your beliefs, maybe even more by my son's father. I believe I was sexually abused by three men. All the men in my life let me down.

My instincts at that moment were to care and ensure the safety of my children and to care for my sick daughter. I wanted to be loved. I wondered what that would feel like. I wondered how it would look like to be truly valued, respected, and honored.

I reflected on my life, and at one point, I decided that enough was enough. I refused to allow any more pain in my life. I had enough of feeling hopelessness, frustration, sadness, helplessness, and pain. I tried leaving him, but I didn't have the support of family or the financial means to support myself; I was tired of not being able to support my family on my own.

I decided to do whatever it takes to graduate high school, something I had put back in the burner because of my circumstances. I got tired—tired of living and accepting the life that I was handed, tired of having to put up with my status quo, tired of being a victim. I became accountable for my consequences and mistakes and took charge of my circumstances.

12

Enough

I decided I was no longer going to allow my circumstances dictate my future. I decided that I no longer was the victim of my circumstances and that I had the ability to change my life. So I went back to adult school. Once I went in and viewed all the courses and subjects I needed to know before graduating, I realized that I knew very little.

That following weekend, I went to the local library and rented all the subject books possible and started studying at home. I studied as much as I could while the kids where at school while they were sleeping. It took me three months before I felt confident to go back and get tested for placement of classes.

I was eager and nervous to get it done. My palms where sweaty as I handed both my tests. I waited patiently outside with the fear of having to take lower grade classes.

The counselor called me in, I came into his office, and he asked me to sit. My heart was honestly racing.

"You are ready to take your exam to receive your GED certificate," the counselor said.

"What? I don't think you realize that I came here for placement of classes and that the last time I finished a grade was back in sixth grade," I said.

"Your test scores came in pretty high. Normally we recommend just taking the exam required to graduate with your test scores," the counselor told me.

I scheduled my test before leaving the office, and as soon as I got in my car, I started crying. I just couldn't believe it! It was so validating and rewarding to know that I had potential this whole time. I called my parents to inform them, thinking that they would be proud. But I was so disappointed by their reaction.

I learned to not count on others for encouragement and motivation. If you do and they aren't there for you, there is only one person who can lift you up—you!

From there on, I grabbed on to that moment and held it for as long as possible and redirected all my anger and frustration and unworthiness to something positive—the possibility that all that I was before was just a facade that the people around me painted because of their brokenness, because of their pain, and the unworthiness they felt. I no longer was going to play the character of a victim in my own life. That same year, I made a very difficult decision that took years to receive forgiveness from my father.

My father had been living at my house for a few months after being homeless. He had now become addicted to crack, the nightmare drug everyone fears. I received a telephone call from the hospital. My sister answered the call, and immediately, she was hysterical, screaming, "My father is dead! My father is dead!" I grabbed the phone from her and talked to the nurse.

He had been shot in the face, the party was at large, and the police were still searching for the suspects. It was a drug deal gone wrong; the drug dealers who shot my father were hoping to kill my father. The hospital staff needed a family member to immediately present themselves at the hospital as he was in critical condition, and the likelihood of him surviving a gunshot to the head was nothing short of a miracle.

All my siblings arrived at the hospital—this time, I got to see the anguish and worry that my mother experienced the day they told her I was in a car accident and in critical condition. At this moment, the feeling of guilt for hating my father came to light, and I realized I hated *his* actions and not *him*. I prayed that my father would be healed that night. More than anything, I prayed for healing on our family.

He had several surgeries, but the doctors couldn't remove the bullet from his head. The bullet entered through his jaw and landed on his nasal socket and was too close to his eye for it to be removed.

My father had reconstructive jaw surgery, and the bullet remains in his nasal socket today.

A few months forward, he began to use drugs again—this time, mixed with the painkillers he was receiving from his doctors. He became delusional; he would lock himself in his room for days, talking to himself, yelling profanity and craziness. The threats of him wanting to kill came back, and I was afraid for my children. I asked my husband to take the kids to the park and not come back until I said. I called 911, and I begged them, "Please, this is my father, he needs help. He is not hurting anyone, but he has lost his mind. Please help me take him to a mental hospital."

God must have heard my prayers that day. After two hours of waiting, the police department sent a trained officer for psychotic people. They gave him the choice to go to jail or to a rehabilitation center. He was in the rehabilitation center for a few months.

I no longer cared what my family thought of me. I was simply no longer going to accept that life.

That night was the turning point for his journey to sobriety, and it started by picking up the Bible after he was released from the rehabilitation center. My father stumbled many times before he completely became cleaned. As he became closer and closer to God, he was cleansed and renewed until he no longer needed drugs or alcohol. God had upheld him with His strength; every time he stumbled back to temptation, He would pick him right up until he was finally free from the chains of addictions. My father eventually forgave me for putting him in a drug rehabilitation center.

I knew I deserved a better life; but if there were going to be any massive changes, I needed massive efforts in my life, and it was all up to me to make it happen. I enrolled into real estate classes and started attending them during the night. Eventually I completed the course in 2003 and went into property management. This was just a stepping-stone to what I had promised my fifteen-year-old self back then.

But my husband continued to be abusive physically. I noticed he would spend a lot of time on the computer, so I put a spy application on our computer. To my surprise, he was online dating. I had proof that he was cheating with online dating, so I confronted him, and he beat me that day. The betrayal and pain he caused me were unbearable, but to be honest, I was numb from so much pain and disappointment already. Only a person who has gone through so much pain in their life can understand this.

There is a point in your life where your only reaction is nothing; because you can no longer feel, you lose touch of what a normal reaction should be. You only know how to survive, and so you do what you have always done to survive. My survival was to up and leave.

I picked up just enough clothes for my three children and left the following day to a homeless shelter called Safe Home. I didn't bother asking my family for help because my husband knew where they lived and my family did not support me leaving him. I was at the shelter for two months, and that was very difficult, but it was just what I needed to save enough money and get my own apartment. The location was top secret; nobody knew where I was during this time. I would go to work and back to the shelter, cautious that no one was following.

I would cry at night from the sadness of having my children going through the same thing I went through when I was a kid. But the people of this organization were amazing! So many families were put into safety, and so many lives were saved because of them.

I filed for divorce during this time and had it uncontested. When it was finalized, I was so relieved from it all. I moved into my apartment with very few furniture, but it felt good. I felt empowered. I focused on work and my children. Pretty soon, we were back on our feet, and I finally felt stability.

Some time passed, I received a phone call from my cousin Felix. He had received a call from a case worker out of Riverside, California. One of my cousins, who will not be named, had given birth to a little girl while detained in the county jail. She had refused to give her a name, so at that time, she was named Baby Girl. They were searching for a family member who could take her in. Not one family member was able to take her, so I stepped in and started the process.

I took the classes and even moved to a bigger apartment to accommodate my Baby Girl. I visited her in Riverside County a few times while we waited for the application to get approved. When we finally had placement of her in my home, all my kids where excited. We instantly bonded with her.

Back then, Nevada did not have normalcy in place and the foster system was a mess, to say the least. Normalcy is when you treat the child the same as you would your children so that they feel more at home. For example, if my kids stay at grandma's for a few hours to play while I do groceries, errands, etc., then the foster child can go as well. I was a single mother at the time, and not having normalcy made everything very difficult since I had to have a licensed day care center watch her for even a minute. To make things worse, Baby Girl arrived without a birth certificate and medical insurance or any shot records.

We named her Destiny, and I love her dearly. She started calling me mommy on her own. When I lost my job as a property manager, I had to report it to her social worker; and when I did, they immediately viewed me as incapable to care for her without giving me any options, since I was a single mother. I had no option but to give her back to the system. They firmly stated that I could even lose my other children.

When they came to pick her up, the social workers were cold and firm. I suppose you get jaded. As they grabbed my child, my little girl was calling me *mommy*. I was devastated and brokenhearted, and I felt as if they had stolen a piece of my heart. I was left broken, and so were my children. I mourned as if I had lost a child. I still cry.

I got depressed after losing Destiny, and dating was not an option. I began to feel alone, and the weight of it all became heavy. It was extremely easy to slowly allow my ex-husband back into my life. We got back together and remarried a year after. Three months right after, I gave birth to my daughter.

Subconsciously, I was doing the same thing my mother did for the longest time, but I had changed. I had grabbed on to hope and faith. I wasn't going to let go of that. I had gone into war with my obstacles. I had gone into war with every single negative judgment, words, predictions, experiences anyone had ever done or said to me.

13

Journey through Grieving

I needed to grieve on everything that had ever happened to me in order for me to heal and move one. There was a part of my life where that was all I did for almost a year. I needed to get all those feelings I held down, pushed down, and suppressed out of my system, in order to transform my life.

Death is often seen as a very negative thing, but we need to remember that death is nearly an illusion because it is part of the process of transformation, ascending, and rebirth. By grieving, you are admitting in a way of the death of something or mourning and accepting a transformation of a new beginning. In my case, it was the acceptance of everything I had been through, and it allowed myself to go through the healing process.

I needed to have compassion for myself and make myself understand that "Hey, you are human! And yes, you are strong, but you have every right to cry, and there is nothing wrong with that." I was angry at a lot of people for what they did to me. Having anger toward them only made me feel worse. It's toxic to harvest feelings of resentment and anger toward anyone. Instead, I slowly started to accept that everything that happened to me has made me into a stronger person. After all, I am still standing here, and whatever they did physically to me only made me a stronger and more resilient being.

The feeling of anger changed into an immense feeling of sadness for what my childhood was like—mostly lonely, dark, and scary. As I raised my children and saw how different my life had been compared to my children, it only made me into a more loving, compassionate mother and human that I am today, knowing that I had control over what their childhood can be like.

I could never change my past nor would I ever change it. I accepted my past as it has molded me in to the "flawsome" person that I am today. With all the wonderful and yet painful flaws that I have, that has given me an opportunity to see right through a person's eyes and truly understand them and have an unconditional love and acceptance for people. I believe that accepting our past trials as past trophies and seeing ourselves as warriors instead give us an opportunity to become stronger and love others for who they truly are. Accepting everything about myself—including my imperfections, my flaws, my shortcomings, and my past—gave me peace and self-validation. I no longer need to be validated by others to feel my worth, and that is truly amazing.

There is no stronger validation than self-validation. It is then that I understood that I am worthy, I am valuable, I am human, and I am loved. I understood that most of my circumstances were out of my control and they were not my fault and that my depression, my feelings, PTSD, and everything that came with the consequences of my traumatic events were validated.

Not only that but because I was able to take my suffering and direct it toward the positive, I could feel and see someone truly hurting and then stop and think twice and lend out my hand to them. I can connect to them and say, "I understand, I was there too." Hearing those words is gold when you are at rock bottom.

We always hear the term "You are strong," but rarely do we hear "You have the right to be weak once in a while." Feeling like you can't go on does not mean you won't ever get up and continue anymore. It just means you need to find time to grieve because it is a natural process for healing. Your soul and your emotions need the rest, just like your body needs rest.

I might never find closure on my sexual assault from when I was five years old, but I must come to terms with that and accept that I might never find closure. The hardest part of my life was the not knowing who committed the assault and the lack of validation on this event from my family.

One of the best things I have ever done was to build a relationship with Jesus Christ. There is no greater peace in knowing that it all works out for a greater purpose and there is no pain, no sacrifice, no tear unnoticed under the Lord's eyes. The intimate and unconditional love and strength He provided through my journey is truly amazing and nothing short of a miracle.

14

Path to Healing

Even though I sometimes had no control over my circumstances, I still had control over who I was, how I felt, and who I was going to become; and nobody could take that away from me. I no longer had fear. I was relentless in becoming who I wanted to become.

I began reading every single book out there on personal development as if I were still chasing the image of that man that once said to me I had to finish high school. But who I was really chasing was my higher self. The book that truly helped me the most is the same book that has been around for almost two thousand years—the Bible.

I took every single one of my tragedies and turned them into experiences that sharpened my character and strengthened my faith. I know now how valuable my experiences truly are just like it was explained in James 1 of the Bible:

> Consider it pure joy, my brothers and sisters, whenever you face trials of many kinds, because you know that the testing of your faith produces perseverance. Let perseverance finish its work so that you may be mature and complete, not lacking anything. (James 1:2–4 NIV)

I also know that it is not an easy process to transform bad experiences into something good. My sexual assaults still haunt me to this day. It's a scar that will probably always hurt. But I refuse to let it be in vain. I became a counselor at a rape crisis center that helped with coping with my own tragedy by being able to help others in such a tragic moment in their life.

But it is not until you discover your purpose when you truly realize the value of turning your failures into something positive. "To appoint unto them that mourn in Zion, to give unto them *beauty for ashes* [my emphasis], the oil of joy for mourning, the garment of praise for the spirit of heaviness; that they might be called trees of righteousness, the planting of the LORD, that he might be glorified," Isaiah 61:3 (KJV) says.

God tells us in this verse to give Him your hurt, brokenness, disappointments, and problems and He will give you beauty in return. Why do I give God the credit for my transformation and my relentless spirit to never give up? Because I had no role model, I had all odds, I had no education, I had no solid foundation, I had nothing but faith—a few seeds were planted in me.

Back when I was fifteen, a seed was planted in me. It was an idea that I could become someone successful. Then it was watered by jumping in by faith and enrolling back in school. I had very little positive experiences and not many role models growing up. But I held on to that moment, and by faith and nothing else, I pursued it. The second seed was when I accepted God into my life and immediately had a feeling of peace and an overwhelming feeling of love that was just poured over my body and soul as if God wanted to give me all the love that was ever denied to me.

I went full time as real estate sales agent and did everything I was taught. I was determined to make it big; however, God had bigger plans for me. Pretty soon, we found ourselves having a team. I found the need to make them accountable and started learning everything on coaching. I honestly loved coaching; it was fulfilling, but it also became an important tool to my success in the future. I ran my ex-husband's real estate team and transactions from home while I was very much pregnant and kept him accountable with marketing updates and new lead generation systems and technology.

If you are seeking a breakthrough, it is nearly impossible to accomplish it without faith. I say *nearly* because I believe nothing is impossible. I had the faith that everything would work out. I found my strength at the cross. I gave everything to God—every single life experience, every single tragedy, and every single disappointment, I gave it all.

I heard a sermon once that you can never change your past, and this is true. But I know someone who could change the course of things and could change the outcome of things, almost to the point as if He had changed the past. This is what God has done for me and my family.

I turned around and saw my father, and I noticed that my father had a miraculous transformation in his life, this transformation was still happening before my eyes! It was not a sudden change; it happened over time, little by little. It started while he was in the storm battling his own demons, long before he was saved. I would often hear my father reading the Bible in the bathroom and in his room while he was having withdrawal moments. I can only imagine how dark his life must have been.

He began reading the scriptures more and more after he was shot in the head, and then slowly after he was released from the rehabilitation center, he began to go to church. The same friend with whom he would often get high ended up being his way to salvation. He often had setbacks, but overtime, he continued to allow God to work in his life.

I noticed that his words changed to positive and encouraging words, and his love for us was now expressed by his actions. My father is not the same man in that room who tried to set the house on fire and abused my mother. I believe in the power of forgiveness and redemption through Christ because I saw my father transform from someone I hated to love and pitied to a father I always dreamed of. My father became a pastor, and his testimony is impactful to many.

My mother was changing as well, seeing my father completely change into someone for whom she only hoped gave her peace and made her curious about the God he was serving. My mother's bitter life had held her back from giving love and having compassion for others, but soon she became more emotionally available. She now owned her home and was financially stable; her love and emotional support that was once void was now full, and it poured not only onto me but onto her grandchildren. She flourished because she no longer lived in fear.

When my brother JP had breakdowns and fell back into drugs, we continued to pray and encourage him with the faith that he would indeed change. Everyone has their own path to healing, and not one single person is the same. One day he realized that he had no other option but to turn his life around or his child was going to end up in the foster system. He was also restored, but this was all done through faith! And I truly believe that it was a product of all the words of encouragement he was now hearing, along with seeing the testimony of our own father.

Accepting, forgiving, and loving my family were only made possible through the agape love that God shows us to have toward each other. The hardest part was my mother forgiving herself for the many things that happened. I understood then how much pain she felt for not being emotionally capable of so many things. She herself was a victim of it all. So I remained in faith, and I held on to this idea that we had the power to become what we hoped for—not alone in my power but with the power of God, in faith.

We are reminded of this faith in the Word: "'For I know the plans I have for you,' declares the Lord, 'plans to prosper you and not to harm you, plans to give you hope and a future'" (Jer. 29:11).

15

Taking Control

I refused to accept lower standards, and instead of taking them in as negative experiences, I took that as fuel to ignite me into improving myself and not so that I can prove anyone otherwise but to prove to myself that I was worthy. I am worthy because He who lives in me says I am worthy. My experiences only built my character and transformed and opened my mind by forcing me to look at people and events at a deeper level and not just superficially.

We may not always be in control of our circumstances, but we are in control on how we react.

I was fired from my husband's own company for not accepting unethical behavior from the broker. I was told I was just an agent, and of that, they were correct. On paper, I was just an agent. But I was not going to accept anyone to downgrade my character and my spirit, and most importantly, I was not ever going to have any agent be treated that way. I picked up my dignity from the conference table surrounded by wolves and walked out with my head held high while my husband remained seated as if he were my enemy.

"She is clothed in strength and dignity, and she laughs without fear of the future," Proverbs 31:25 says. I had been down this beaten path before. I have picked up my dignity and strength from nothing before when my bottom fell through, and I only knew how to do one thing well—continue to fight. So I did.

I dusted off the bitterness, hate, and resentfulness. All my experiences had built my character, but it was because I was deeply connected with God and allowed for a transformation to come in as I searched for wisdom, strength, and knowledge in every hurt, every brokenness, and every lost hope. Had I not searched for the knowledge and guidance through my divine God, I would have missed out on the lesson and wisdom behind; and I would not be as wise as I am now. Yet I still have so much to learn and so much to work on. But I'm stronger, and I know that I can trust that all things work out in the end.

After that, I went back to doing what I knew best—reading, studying, and improving myself. I focused on the four main things everyone and anyone needs to focus on in order to have massive success and breakthrough. After all, this is what I was teaching myself to real estate agents:

Spirituality
Physical
Mental
Emotional

I started doing CrossFit during the time I was discharged from my husband's company. I took time to really focus in having a closer connection with God, so I did Bible study once a week and did worship throughout the day. I also started journaling; I did my "Gratitudes and Affirmations" journal almost every day during this time, along with my written goals. A few years later, I found my old book and noticed I had accomplished my goals. I can tell you that by focusing on these four aspects of myself worked miracles in all areas of my life. For what you water, with time, sprouts. I studied many successful people, and they all had one thing in common: they all excelled in all those areas in life.

I think back now, and I thank everyone for firing me from that awful environment in my husband's company. I thank all the people who said no to me and the ones who said I wasn't going to amount to much in life. Because of them, I would have never known what I am truly capable of today. I am capable of true forgiveness and unconditional love for myself and for others. I am capable of compassion and uplifting others through this book, and it is because of my bad experiences that shaped who I am today. It was a blessing in disguise.

How many blessings in disguise do we truly have?

"For the Lord your God is he who goes with you to fight for you against your enemies, to give you the victory," Deuteronomy 20:4 says.

After, being fired from that brokerage and going to work for someone with loose screws in their head, I decided that perhaps God was pointing to something better for me. "Whether you turn to the right or to the left, your ears will hear a voice behind you, saying *'This is the way; walk in it* [my emphasis],'" Isiah 30:21 reminded me.

I took a deep breath and jumped in by faith with the bare minimal amount to open a brokerage. I had nothing—no leads, no agents, and just one listing for which I still had to fight. I was relying solely on my faith. Everything started coming together. Deals were coming through; I slowly started getting more and more agents. Then I finally hit it big. I closed my first big transaction. It seemed as if all the hard work and perseverance finally paid off and I was now on top of the world.

But if had not listened to the direction I was being pulled or if I had lacked faith, all this would have never happened. I had six children, I lacked resources, and the whole time, I wasn't very well known in the industry as I was always working behind the curtains. But I was tired of being beat down, so when the owner of the company I worked for decided to take my multimillion-dollar deal, I had already been beat down so many times that instead of me sitting crying in the corner like he expected, he lit a fire in my belly that made me pull out my claws and fight for what was righteously mine.

My experiences in life had molded me into becoming a natural leader and sharpened my character so I can defend and help others achieve their personal dreams and goals. However, this only happens if you pay attention to the lesson each failure and season has in your life. Working with investors and multimillionaires in the industry, I had the luxury to ask them very private things. Mainly, I was curious about how they became successful and if they truly had a fulfilling life.

Here is something you don't want to hear: they had many failures, they were scared to death all the time, they jumped and made the big decision, and they lost loved ones on their way to success because they did not support them. To my surprise, they lived a very discontent and unfulfilling life. Very few managed to have the best of both worlds.

You see, the meaning of success became media driven. We lost touch of what the meaning of success truly is, and so it became a money-chasing frenzy that ultimately leaves you in an unfulfilling life at the end of your years. You look back and realize that you had only one god—and it was money. You lost the love of your life and remarried again and again, only to realize that neither were the true causes of your marriage failures; it was because your priorities were out of alignment. Perhaps you remained married, only to turn around and realize that your kids are now grown and now you are all alone and never got to enjoy them because your meetings and deadlines were the priority. So at the end of your life, you have all this money but no one to share it with.

Whatever the case is, what you focus on will eventually saturate your life. Balance is the key to true success! You must search for what brings you peace, fulfillment, and purpose then make money the side product of that. Then you will realize that retirement doesn't come at the end of your years when you are too old to do anything anyway! Instead, you will find that retirement comes the day you realize what your purpose is and then find a way to make money doing what your purpose is.

When I discovered my purpose in life, everything just clicked and came together for me. I knew that in order to live a successful life, I needed to do what I am purposed on this earth to do—and that is to give my testimony in order save, uplift, and inspire others to never give up and find comfort in Jesus Christ who is our Lord and Savior.

I had been drawn closer to fostering kids, and this whole time, I didn't really understand why. But now I do. I wanted to help the child who didn't get help, the same as that little girl I once was. My spiritual awakening started with one decision—getting connected with God. My determination to change my circumstances followed with one question, *Should I continue to be the victim or should I decide to rise above my circumstances?*

It is very easy to be the victim in any situation, but the consequences of that are devastating. I decided to fight; I decided to see myself worthy of obtaining the things I truly wanted. I had already seen and lived in hell and darkness; I wanted desperately to see the light.

But we often don't feel the need to grow unless we are uncomfortable enough and enclosed in darkness.

"She's been through hell and came out, an angel. You didn't break her, darling. You don't own that kind of power," as BMM Poetry says. In order to do so, I needed to raise my standards of who I was and what I was going to allow in my life. "She is more precious than rubies; nothing you desire can compare with her," Proverbs 3:15 reminded me. The times I found myself broken and tired, I clinched to the cross. "I can do all things through him who strengthens me," Philippians 4:13 says.

So easily do we give up in faith, after not hearing our prayers answered, not understanding that everything works in perfect timing and not on our own schedule. So many times the events throughout my life happened at the exact moment they needed to happen, and deliverance came when least expected.

16

Ashes for Beauty

The very fact that I made it to this country and received amnesty was a blessing and full of opportunities. The day I received US citizenship was one of the best days of my life.

The opportunities that this country provides are simply limitless. Even though I was still discriminated in so many ways and will most likely continue to be one way or another, I still can stand up for myself and demand justice and receive it. The journey to this wonderful country was perfect timing!

I reflect back; and I see either so many things that matured me, built my character, and gave me wisdom and experience or I could very well go back and simply call them tragedies (empty tragedies). I refuse to leave my life experiences just as tragedies. We are after all creators of our own life for God created us in His image. Thus, we are creators. We can decide if we allow certain things to discourage us, break us, hurt us, or define us. Or we can set our standards and define ourselves and decide what we allow to break us and hurt us and how we view our failures, tragedies, and experiences. I read once in a book, a quote from Holocaust survivor Viktor E. Frankl, "There is only one thing that I dread: not to be worthy of my sufferings."

Consequently, after understanding my worth, I came to the conclusion that if I truly wanted to live a better life and value myself for who I am truly worth, then I needed to get a divorce. This decision was not easy—and it wasn't like I just threw in the towel—but it was one of the best decisions in my life.

Viewing life now on my own is challenging but I am not afraid. I've done this before, once upon a time. Only this time, I know my worth.

Whether you are a child in the foster system or a single mother struggling to feed your children or perhaps you are in an abusive situation at the moment or you are fighting a disease—you have hope and you are worthy of so much more. I want you to look and search for that one moment in your life when you felt extreme joy or hope. Hang on to that moment; use it and let it really soak in. Because even though things get really tough at times and you can't seem to find a solution, God says there is nothing new under the sun. What you are going through right now this moment, there is somebody out there who has gone through it and overcame it.

Find your worth because you are worthy—very much worthy and loved.

Here is a reflection that actually happened to me not too long ago, and it taught me a valuable lesson:

> I was talking to God on my way driving home. I was making my case on how nobody ever loved me and how He couldn't possibly love me either.
>
> My case was good; I had great points. Since I was little, I've been through hell and back, and now again in a few weeks I will face the world alone.
>
> Then there was a young man walking on the street with no shirt, just shorts and ripped sandals, and his hair covered in dirt.
>
> He was holding a small pile—his entire belongings on his hand. He looked like he had not showered in months.
>
> My heart broke down as I noticed the world ignored this man.
>
> I stopped, and I asked him if he would like new shoes and clothes. But he declined, saying he was just fine but could use some food.

Without hesitation, I grabbed him some food. He kept walking as if it was too good to be true; so it took me a while to find him when I came back with Subway and a large drink.

He was extremely grateful and polite. Then out of nowhere, I heard a voice say, "*Tell him I love him,*" so I told the man, "God wants you to know that He loves you."

He said, "Thank you, ma'am."

I choked on my tears, and then I realized if God loves this man, then what makes me think God doesn't love me?

In a world full of hurt, we can forget how loved we are.

Give compassion and love to a stranger because that is God's way of showing love to us.

—GG

You are loved, and because you are loved, that must mean you are worthy! Find your strength, but in order to get the kind of strength, you will need to overcome your situation—you first have to learn to forgive.

17
Letting Go

It wasn't easy for me to forgive every single person who has ever hurt me, but I started with the easiest to forgive. Then I kept gathering courage and strength to forgive everyone else. I forgave my mother for everything she didn't do for me and everything she did. Then my brother, then my sister, followed by my father. I eventually forgave all my assaulters. I learned I also had to forgive myself.

Forgiveness became easier once I learned what it truly means and removed old beliefs of what others think it means:

Forgiveness is not forgetting—you will always remember what happened and how it felt.

Forgiveness is not reconciliation—reconciliation is a something that happens with the efforts between two or more persons, not based solely on your action.

Forgiveness is not a onetime thing—you may remember again and end up feeling the pain when the person who hurt you reminds you or an event reminds you, and all those feelings will come back. This is what I mean by forgiving again:

Forgiveness is letting go of all resentment and hate toward that person.

> Resentment and hate is such a heavy bag to be carrying around. It drags and tires your soul. You should always remember that you are choosing to forgive so that you can have a better life.
>
> *Forgiveness is the hammer that shatters one's walls to allow the soul to become free and love unconditionally.*
>
> —GG

First, you must know your purpose. We all have a purpose in this world, but for many years, I actually thought I didn't have one. My purpose was revealed only after I was connected with my higher self; by this, I mean with my faith and beliefs in Jesus. In your spiritual growth and healing is where you really find yourself, getting to know the inner you and what your passions are.

The truth of the matter is that we will always have obstacles and challenges in life. But we must find the beauty within our challenges in order to accept the truth learn and continue moving forward. The challenge is in your perspective. The challenge is never the problem but *how* you manage the problem.

Perhaps the biggest lesson here is to have courage above all:

> the courage to forgive,
> the courage to take that first step,
> the courage to leave that bad relationship,
> the courage to voice your opinion,
> the courage to show your true colors,
> the courage to free yourself from stereotypes,
> the courage to love yourself just as you are,
> the courage to feel beautiful in your own skin,
> the courage to take on that new challenge,
> the courage to be opened and susceptible to new love in your life, and
> the courage to love back and be vulnerable.

Receiving love when it's hitting us straight on the face is always the hardest when we have built walls, brick by brick, after every failed relationship. This is why it is so important to forgive, accept, and let go. It has always been about you and not about the other party. We forgive to allow ourselves to love and be loved because we are worthy of something beautiful. We must have courage to allow love in our lives.

I don't mean be vulnerable and have your guard down. We all know when real love is in front of us. Being vulnerable to allow love in versus being vulnerable and letting someone hurt you are two different things.

So I encourage you to persevere and fight the good fight and remain hopeful and confident that all things work out for those who have faith. The Word in 1 Timothy 6:12 tells us, "Fight the good fight of faith, lay hold on eternal life, to which you were also called and have confessed the good confession in the presence of many witnesses" (NKJV).

To all my colleagues and friends who are entrepreneurs—I say that your goals are not big enough, if you have set your goals only on the material realm of this world, which will exist one day and the next disappear. For what good is all you have if you have not set your eye on the ultimate prize at hand?

Just remember what Philippians 3:13–14 tells us:

> Brethren, I do not count myself to have apprehended; but one thing *I do,* forgetting those things which are behind and reaching forward to those things which are ahead, I press toward the goal for the prize of the upward call of God in Christ Jesus. (NKJV)

—With all love,
GG

www.ingramcontent.com/pod-product-compliance
Lightning Source LLC
Chambersburg PA
CBHW021451070526
44577CB00002B/352